NEW AGE
MASQUERADE

JONATHAN WELTON

New Age Masquerade
Copyright © 2014— Jonathan Welton

All rights reserved. This book is protected by the copyright laws of the United States of America. This book may not be copied or reprinted for commercial gain or profit. The use of short quotations or occasional page copying for personal or group study is permitted and encouraged. Permission will be granted upon request.

Unless otherwise identified, Scripture quotations are taken from the THE HOLY BIBLE, NEW INTERNATIONAL VERSION®, NIV®. Copyright © 1973, 1978, 1984, 2010 by Biblica, Inc.™ www.xulonpress.com. Emphasis within Scripture quotations is the author's own. Scripture quotations marked NASB are taken from the NEW AMERICAN STANDARD BIBLE®, Copyright © 1960,1962,1963,1968,1971,1972, 1973,1975,1977,1995 by The Lockman Foundation. Used by permission. Scripture quotations marked NLT are taken from the Holy Bible, New Living Translation, copyright 1996, 2004. Used by permission of Tyndale House Publishers., Wheaton, Illinois 60189. All rights reserved. Scripture quotations marked NKJV are taken from the New King James Version. Copyright © 1982 by Thomas Nelson, Inc. Used by permission. All rights reserved. Scripture quotations marked ESV are taken from The Holy Bible, English Standard Version® (ESV®), copyright © 2001 by Crossway, a publishing ministry of Good News Publishers. Used by permission. All rights reserved.

All definitions of New Age terms are taken from *The Element Encyclopedia of the Psychic World* by Theresa Cheung (London: HarperElement, 2006).

Jon Welton Ministries
P.O. Box 92126
Rochester, NY 14692
http://www.weltonacademy.com/

ISBN: 978-0-615-96672-4
Printed in the United States of America

Acknowledgements

***Jacqueline Frattare**—Without your constant poking and prodding, this manuscript wouldn't have been completed. Your hunger and passion to see those caught in earth-based religions come to know the glorious light of Jesus has inspired me to keep on until this was completed. It is my hope that this book will not only offend the religious and break God out of the boxes we have put Him in, but also that many lost will see the light. Jaci, for all the souls that will be impacted by this book, you also share in that reward.

Contents

Foreword   Patricia King

Part One: The Foundation

Chapter 1   Understanding the New Age Movement
Chapter 2   Authentic Versus Counterfeit
Chapter 3   Power Encounters and the Old Testament
Chapter 4   New Testament Power Encounters

Part Two: The Supernatural

Introduction
Chapter 5   Elements of the Spirit Realm

> *Affirmations • Age of Aquarius • Akashic Records, the Book of the Dead • Astral Body • Astral Plane • Astrology • Aura • Disciplines • Elements • Elementals • Fasting/Eating • Guided Visualization • Home Circle • Imagination • Initiation Rites • Invocation or Evocation • Karma • Meditation • Necromancy • New Age • Numerology • Prayer • Silver Cord • Smudging • Spirit Guide • Trances • Universal Life Force*

CHAPTER 6   Spiritual Insight

Channeling • Clairaudience • Clairsentience • Clairvoyance • Cold Reading • Death Omen • Displacement • Divination • Dowsing • Dream Interpretation • Extrasensory Perception (ESP) • Horoscope • Hot Reading • Precognition or Premonition • Prophecy • Psychic Art • Remote Viewing • Retrocognition • Tapping into Ancient Truths • Vision • Zodiac

CHAPTER 7   Other Phenomenon

Absent Healing • Apport • Automatic Writing • Body Work • Earthquake Effect • Ectoplasm • Guardian Spirit or Angel • Incorruptibility • Levitation • Miracles • Orbs • Out-of-Body Experience (OBE) • Power Objects • Power Spots • Psychic Healing • Shape Shifting • Spirit Attachment and Releasement • Telekenesis • Teleportation • Temporal Displacement • Zombies

CONCLUSION

Foreword
By Patricia King

Before coming to Christ, I had joined a number of New Age groups. I was spiritually hungry, looking for a power greater than myself, and searching for answers to the confused life I was living. I discovered that those I met in the New Age community were of the same heart. We were searching for God, yet all we discovered were energies, vibes, spiritual exercises, and "illuminations" that promised to "tune us in" to what we needed to live in the highest of spiritual frequencies and light. We constantly listened to the lectures of various teachers and gurus, who claimed their insights would transform our lives.

All those I met in the various expressions of New Age culture were as sincere as I was in our search for truth and enlightenment, but I soon discovered we were all sincerely wrong. We had been deceived. Every practice promised so much, yet delivered so little. Although the beginning of the journey was full of anticipation, it became old quickly. We certainly had exciting moments, as we discovered and experienced various encounters with spiritual force and energy, but all the while, my heart was looking for something much deeper. I was looking for the truth that would set me free. I was searching for God.

After I came to Christ, the Lord revealed to me the treachery of the deception I had walked in, and as a result, I renounced my association with those practices and received much needed deliverance ministry. I continued to love my friends in the New Age community; they were all very caring people and were also in search of the truth. I had opportunities to share the gospel with many of them. The thief comes to kill, steal, and destroy (see John 10:10), and he will always try to keep us from the true by offering us a counterfeit. The New Age practices could never lead me to what I was searching for—my Savior, my God.

New Agers, gurus, and witches were my precious friends when I lived in that stream, but after I came to Christ, I detected great fear in the Body toward people like them. I heard, in reaction to this fear, many Christians make strong judgments against New Agers and issue severe warnings to other believers, exhorting them to avoid the "witches" at all costs. It was confusing to me. How could the God of love, who had rescued me from lies and deceptions, not want to love and rescue them, too?

As I walked with Christ, I discovered authentic spiritual truth in the Scriptures that was very life-transforming. I came to realize that most of what I experienced within the New Age community contained some threads of truth, but the source was a counterfeit spirit, and therefore, much of it was distorted. Some of the principles and revelations were in line with Scripture, but they had no connection with the true and living God. There is only *one name* under heaven by which people can be saved, and that is Jesus Christ (see Acts 4:12). He is the way, the truth, and the life, and *no one* can come to the Father except through Him (see John 14:6).

Jonathan Welton has done a tremendous job writing *New Age Masquerade*. In it, he brilliantly discloses the biblical foundations that have been counterfeited in specific New Age practices. The enemy has taken scriptural truth, twisted it, and dangled it before the spiritually hungry. He knows all people were created for encounter with God, and his goal is to draw people away from Jesus and to himself by using the very things we were made to embrace. Remember, if there

Foreword

is a counterfeit, there must be an authentic. In *New Age Masquerade*, Jonathan will introduce you to the authentic.

In no way is this book meant to invite the reader to embrace New Age practices or the deceptive roots that lie beneath those practices. This book has been written to reveal the truth that the enemy used to produce the counterfeit. Expert discerners of counterfeit currency are not trained to study the counterfeit. They are trained to study the authentic. They become so familiar with the authentic that when a counterfeit is presented, they discern it immediately. Oh, that we, the Church, would be that discerning through knowing the truth in fullness.

We are living in a spiritual revolution, and God is delivering His people from holding to a form of godliness and denying the power. We, as lovers of Jesus Christ, are being invited to embrace the supernatural without fear. *New Age Masquerade*, by Jonathan Welton, will help you grow in discernment and in confidence to pursue God in all His fullness. The teachings in the book will also help you relate better to the spiritually hungry who are not yet in Christ. They are searching for Him, although they might not yet be aware that He is the one their souls long for.

Read this book, draw close to God and all He is offering you in this hour, and then *go* and reach others for His glory. He died so that they might have life! *Go* in His love and in His truth.

Part One
The Foundation

Chapter 1

Understanding the New Age Movement

I have a bookshelf in my home that my friends and family humorously refer to as my "evil shelf." As I have personally researched the material in this book over five years, I have gathered books from movements such as the New Age, Wicca, Paganism, and Satanism. On my evil shelf, I keep books with titles such as *Occult Preparations for the New Age, Talking to the Dead,* and *Lucifer Rising.* Basically, books most orthodox Bible-believing Christians would never read or allow in their homes.

I knew that my evil shelf had gotten a little out of control when my friend Adam called me and excitedly announced over the phone, "I am at the bookstore and they have this huge *Witchcraft Encyclopedia* on clearance for $5.99 and I thought of you! Should I get it for you?"

After a long pause, I hesitantly said yes and hung up. *This might be the weirdest phone call I have ever received as a good little Christian author!* I thought to myself.

Having grown up in legalistic Pentecostalism, I know well the paranoia about having occult books in my home. I had the cassette tapes that claim all rock music is satanic, and I read those terrible Chick Publications. No worries. I am up to speed on Christian superstition.

Since I am called to write this book, I believe in the power of the Holy Spirit to protect me in the process. When I bring a new book home for my evil shelf, the first thing I do is drop it on the floor and put my foot on top of it and declare, "You will not mess with the spiritual atmosphere of my home; you are here for research only, and I am the authority in this house." Then I put it on my shelf and sleep soundly without any problem.

As I have researched, I have noticed a common misconception among Christians—that there is no difference between New Age, Witchcraft, and Satanism. This leads to a major problem in communication. For example, when people say they are into New Age, Christians seem to categorize them among witches and child sacrifice rituals, which is extremely exaggerated and disrespectful.

Instead, I have found it helpful to think of the New Age, Wicca, Animism, and Satanism as different streams of earth-based religion, each with their own unique history and distinctions. Similarly, Christianity has many denominations. Imagine a New Ager talking with a Lutheran and saying, "So basically, you are the same as a Catholic, right? You are all Christians, so what's the difference?" Clearly, anyone who is a Christian recognizes the huge differences between Catholics and Lutherans, and many would even be offended by this generalization, Martin Luther included. The same applies to those in earth-based religions.

For this reason, we must understand the basic differences if we want to have clear, inoffensive, intelligent conversations with those in earth-based religions. I will begin with a simple overview of four different streams: Animism, Wicca, New Age, and Satanism. Then I will examine the history of the New Age movement, as it is the one stream I will be focused on in the majority of this book.

Animism

According to *The Element Encyclopedia of the Psychic World*:

> At the root of magic beliefs and practice, animism is the belief that every natural object, both living and non-living, has a spirit or life force....The animist sees movement in trees, rocks, streams, wind and other objects and believes that everything is inhabited by its own spirit.[1]

Animism is behind the concept that if it does not rain and the crops fail the "rain spirit" must be displeased and we must, therefore, offer a sacrifice to appease him. This basic belief system is behind the ancient pagan polytheistic societies that lived as victims of the many angry and warring gods. Only the powerful Shamans (witchdoctors) knew how to use rituals, curses, and healing potions. Michael Harper has written extensively about this belief system in his groundbreaking work, *The Way of the Shaman*. Yet Animism is rarely observed in regions impacted by monotheism, such as Europe, Russia, and North America.

Wicca

The Witch Book: The Encyclopedia of Witchcraft, Wicca, and Neo-Paganism says:

> Wicca is the preferred word for "Witchcraft" with most Witches today, since it does not carry the negativity associated with the stereotypical witch promoted by Christianity. It denotes the positive, nature-oriented Pagan religion derived from pre-Christian roots.[2]

Similarly, New Age author and lecturer Silver Ravenwolf writes:

> Witchcraft is an earth-centered religion focused on raising an individual's spirituality. Witchcraft is not, nor was it ever, a vehicle for Satanic worship.[3]

Wiccans generally have a lot in common with Animists. Interestingly, Wicca denies the existence of an individual spirit known as the devil. Therefore, they resent the way many Christians lump Witchcraft and Satanism together. Within Witchcraft/Wicca exists a range from white magic to black magic. Both can involve spells, potions, rituals, and incantations, yet the purpose is different. A "love potion" would be considered white magic, whereas a hex and a curse of death would be considered black magic. Black magic can be so common in some circles that books have been written about how to defend oneself against psychic attacks, such as Dion Fortune's book, *Psychic Self-Defense*.

NEW AGE

Trying to define the New Age movement is a very difficult challenge. The basic concept is that the world has entered a spiritual Age of Enlightenment, and through self-improvement and personal empowerment, human perfection and tranquility can be found. If a Creator God exists, all paths of love will lead us to Him or Her. The New Age is like a patchwork quilt made of pieces from ancient shamanism, Paganism, Wicca, eastern mysticism, and reincarnation. This blended philosophy has no formal structure and is highly individualized. The main goal is typically to be a better person and have a better society without the restrictions that traditional religions would bring.

Satanism

This category hardly deserves to be put alongside Animism, Wicca, and the New Age, as these three are very different from Satanism. However, I include it here because Christianity has typically lumped them all together, and I would like to bring clarity to this error.

Satanism's core value is to be the antithesis of Christianity. Without Christianity, there is no Satanism. Satanism takes all the ordinances of Christianity, "Thou shalt not," and turns them into "thou shalt." It is chaos, destruction, anarchy, and disorder in its purest form as a religion. It gained a major upsurge through the writings and practices of Aleister Crowley and was institutionalized by Anton LaVey when he founded the Church of Satan in San Francisco in 1966. The 1970s and '80s were filled with heavy metal bands and horror films that glamorized Satanism for financial gain. Christians fell right into their trap by protesting and authoring countless books against rock and Satanism. This led to incredible exaggerations of Satanism's power and even to outright fraud, such as the famous Christian comedian Mike Warnke's bestseller, *The Satan Seller*, in which he lied about his background inside Satanism.

With these brief and very basic definitions of Animism, Wicca, the New Age, and Satanism, we can clearly see the vast difference between the first three earth-based religions and Satanism, which is explicitly anti-Christian. It is important to keep this in mind as we look now at the history of the New Age movement and begin to compare it to Christianity.

History of the New Age Movement

The New Age movement was founded by people who were, in some ways, very much like me. I have always been fascinated by the supernatural. Yet as a child raised in a Christian family, I attended a church that didn't talk about or operate much in the supernatural. Because many churches do not talk about the supernatural, many young people like me begin to search it out. For me this meant going to the public library and reading the shelves of ghost stories and supernatural unsolved mysteries. I was captivated. I knew there must be more than the physical universe. I also knew, if the darkness had supernatural power, the God of light must have even more, even if my church didn't talk about it. Just by reading the Bible, I could recognize the supernatural should be natural. It was not reserved for the pastor or the televangelist but was available to every simple follower of God.

As I grew, I discovered an entire movement within the Church distinguished by a belief in God's supernatural power. They believe Christians can experience visions, dreams, supernatural healing, and miracles without being weird or trying to extort money. Immediately, I hungrily began pursuing and walking in the supernatural as a Christian.

I also began to research the New Age movement. I found it fascinating that people without religion were operating in the supernatural. Through my research, I discovered the movement had its beginnings inside Christianity, and only over time did it grow apart. This pattern has repeated itself often; a very high percentage of those in the New Age grew up in Christian families and later left. Their reason for leaving is one that none of us want to hear. Inside the Church, they felt rejected and uncomfortable being supernatural individuals.

Thus, both individual New Agers, as well as the whole history of the movement, started within Christianity and developed out and away from it because the supernatural was unwelcome at church. This is not just a random coincidence. The fact that the six major founders of what has morphed into the modern New Age movement essentially had Christian roots is a sign of something significant. Let's examine these six founders briefly.

Emanuel Swedenborg (1688–1772)

Emanuel Swedenborg is considered by many to be one of the earliest founders of the spiritualist movement, which later became the modern New Age movement. Emanuel's father, Jesper, who came from a wealthy mining family, spent his youth traveling abroad and studying theology. His eloquence earned him favor with the Swedish king, Charles XI, and eventually, through the king's influence, Jesper became a professor of theology at Uppsala University and the Bishop of Skara. However, Jesper aligned himself with the dissenting Lutheran Pietist movement, which eventually caused him to be charged as a heretic. Growing up with a father who wanted to see the Church change its doctrine made a deep impression on Emanuel.

As an adult, Emanuel followed his father's path even farther. His heart intentions seemed good, and some even consider him a Christian mystic. Perhaps, as a Lutheran, he imagined himself to be walking in the very footsteps of the great reformer, Martin Luther. Yet the foundations he laid did not move the Church toward greater health. Instead, he established many unorthodox teachings that eventually became the foundation of spiritualism and the New Age movement. For example, he taught that communication with the dead was a viable source of spiritual information. He also rejected the idea of a final judgment of sin, teaching rather a universal salvation of all people eventually. He placed a higher value on his own dreams and visions than upon the Bible, which is always a slippery slope. As a result, he had no standard for testing his dreams and visions.

In all, Swedenborg wrote eighteen published theological works and several more that were unpublished; his most recognized work is *Heaven and Hell* (first published in Latin in 1758), which has had over fifty-five printings. His teachings influenced such notable individuals as William Blake, Elizabeth Barrett Browning, Ralph Waldo Emerson, Carl Jung, Johnny Appleseed, and Helen Keller.[4]

Franz Anton Mesmer (1734–1815)

Franz Anton Mesmer followed closely on the heels of Swedenborg, although he was more of a scientist than a theologian. He believed a magnetic fluid existed in the human body, and he referred to its effect upon a person as animal magnetism. The "mesmerism" he formulated and practiced in his animal magnetism teachings is the foundation of what has come to be known as hypnosis. Not surprisingly, from his name the word *mesmerize* is derived.

Mesmer was trained under the Jesuits and was very well studied in science for his day. In fact, in 1784, without Mesmer requesting it, King Louis XVI appointed four members of the Faculty of Medicine as commissioners to investigate the animal magnetism theories, including the American ambassador Benjamin Franklin.

I believe Mesmer stumbled across the reality of the spirit realm, yet he approached it as a scientist. Essentially he taught that the human body has an energy that, when unbalanced, causes sickness. Unfortunately, because he tried to speak of spiritual realities as a scientist, he received much ridicule and persecution. If he had looked in the Bible, he might have found Third John 2, which says, *"I pray that you would be in health, even as your soul prospers."* The Bible clearly establishes a very real connection between our health and the state of our souls.

In writing, Mesmer left an eighty-eight-page book on his theory of animal magnetism, which postulated his famous twenty-seven propositions. Yet his most famous contribution to history is his name, which has become associated with the trance-like state of mind referred to as being *mesmerized*.[5]

Andrew Jackson Davis (1826–1910)

Sir Arthur Conan Doyle, author of the *Sherlock Holmes* series, said of Andrew Jackson Davis:

> Davis does not appear to have been at all a religious man in the ordinary conventional sense, although he was drenched with true spiritual power. His views, so far as one can follow them, were very critical as regards Biblical revelation, and, to put it as lowest, he was no believer in literal interpretation.[6]

As Doyle implies, we do not know what Andrew Jackson Davis' interaction with Christianity was. What we do know of Davis is that his views were very clearly built upon the foundation Swedenborg laid. As the story goes, in 1844, Andrew Jackson Davis had an experience that changed the course of his life. On the evening of March 6, Davis was suddenly overcome by a power that led him to "fly" (in the spirit) from Poughkeepsie, where he lived; in a semi-trance state, he hurried off upon a rapid journey. When he regained full consciousness the next morning, he found himself amidst the Catskill Mountains, some forty miles away. There, he claimed to have met two very distinguished men, whom he later identified as the philosopher Galen and the Swedish seer Emanuel Swedenborg, both of whom were, of course, dead. He also claimed to have experienced a great mental illumination and revelation.

Davis was not widely known in his day, yet he was highly influential to the development of the spiritualism movement. He was a follower of Swedenborg, yet he also studied and practiced mesmerism. In 1847, he published *The Principles of Nature, Her Divine Revelations,* and *A Voice to Mankind*, which in 1845 he had dictated while in a trance to his scribe, William Fishbough. He began to tour and lecture, but with very little success, and eventually he returned to writing books as his primary means of teaching, publishing about thirty in all.

It is purported that Davis performed séances for Abraham and Mary Todd Lincoln (the Lincolns were very interested in séances because of the death of their son Willie) and predicted many major inventions. Notably, the following prediction of the automobile was recorded in his book, *The Penetralia* (1856):

> Question: Will utilitarianism make any discoveries in other locomotive directions?
>
> Yes: look out about there days for carriages and traveling saloons on country roads—without horses, without steam, without any visible motive power moving with greater speed and far more safety than at present.
>
> Carriages will be moved by a strange and beautiful and simple admixture of aqueous and atmospheric gases—so easily condensed, so simply ignited, and so imparted by a machine somewhat resembling our engines, as to be entirely concealed and managed between the forward wheels. These vehicles will prevent many embarrassments now experienced by persons living in thinly populated territories. The first requisite for these land locomotives will be good roads, upon which with your engine, without your horses, you may travel with great rapidity. These carriages seem to me of uncomplicated construction.[7]

Davis, who was sometimes called the John the Baptist of spiritualism, also predicted its advent. In his most famous work, *Principles of Nature* (1847), he states:

> It is a truth that spirits commune with one another while one is in the body and the other in the higher spheres—and this, too, when the person in the body is unconscious of the influx, and hence cannot be convinced of the fact; and this truth will ere long present itself in the form of

a living demonstration. And the world will hail with delight the ushering in of that era when the interiors of men will be opened, and the spiritual communion will be established.[8]

One year later, the Fox sisters began hearing the spirit rappings that inaugurated the spiritualism movement. Davis believed this a fulfillment of his prophecy.

Davis was a spiritual descendent of Swedenborg and Mesmer, and Davis in turn directly influenced the psychic, Edgar Cayce (1877–1945), who adopted trance diagnosis and similar activities, with few modifications, from Davis. In fact, Davis' complete library is now housed within the Edgar Cayce Library. Edgar Allan Poe was also inspired by Davis, whose lectures on mesmerism he had attended. This is especially evident in Poe's short story, "The Facts in the Case of M. Valdemar" (1845).[9]

The Fox Sisters

One of the most significant dates in New Age history is March 31, 1848. In Hydesville, New York (now known as Arcadia, twenty miles east of Rochester, New York), a small Methodist family began to hear strange tappings on the inside of their cabin walls. The two younger daughters of the family, Maggie and Kate (ages fifteen and twelve) began to communicate with the tappings by asking yes-or-no questions using a system like "one tap for yes and two taps for no." The girls began to refer to the phenomena as talking to "Mr. Splitfoot," which was a nickname for the then common hoofed depictions of the devil.

"Mr. Splitfoot" told the girls he was the spirit of a traveling peddler who had been killed years before and buried in the basement of their Hydesville home. At this news, their father called in the Methodist pastor for spiritual help. He also gathered the neighbors to help him dig in the basement in search of a body. When they struck water, the dig halted. But many years later, in 1904, a false wall in the basement collapsed, revealing the remains of a man with a peddler's box.[10]

From these young sisters sprang the major expansion of the spiritualist movement. From 1848 to 1888, they essentially toured, taught and demonstrated mediumship all through America, especially the Northeast. Through their demonstrations, the movement began to establish spiritualist churches and even a famed summer camp near Buffalo, New York, named Lily Dale.

Arthur Conan Doyle (1859–1930)

Arthur Conan Doyle was born in Edinburgh, Scotland, on May 22, 1859, into a Roman Catholic family, and he attended Catholic schools. At age seventeen, he began studying medicine at Edinburgh University, eventually earning his doctorate of medicine. While at Edinburgh, he decided he no longer subscribed to the Catholic point of view. About this, he wrote in his autobiography, *Memories and Adventures*:

> I remember that when, as a grown lad, I heard Father Murphy, a great fierce Irish priest, declare that there was sure damnation for everyone outside the church, I looked upon him with horror, and to that moment I trace the first rift which has grown into such a chasm between me and those who were my guides.[11]

As a man of tremendous renown, Sir Arthur Conan Doyle was a strong advocate of the spiritualism movement. Although he was born eleven years after the Hydesville incident with the Fox Sisters, Doyle gave the movement a lot of momentum in its later years. He is most famed for his *Sherlock Holmes* novels, which contained much of the spiritualism he ascribed to. Doyle also made a major contribution to spiritualism by writing, *The History of Spiritualism* (1926).

Around the same time, Harry Houdini, the renowned American illusionist and escape artist, began to debunk many of the fraudulent spiritualists and mediums. At this, Doyle began to regularly communicate with Houdini. He would send Houdini information regarding certain mediums, and Houdini would then expose their tricks. It was not Doyle's goal to see these mediums exposed, as he was a sincere believer in spiritualism. The interactions between these two giants is recorded in amazing detail in the *Final Séance* by Massimo Polidoro.

Arthur Conan Doyle also had an interaction with the famous Pentecostal healer John G. Lake. In Lake's own words:

> Finally a meeting was arranged between Sir Oliver Lodge, Sir Arthur Conan Doyle, W.T. Stead, and myself. I want to say a word concerning these two great men. Both have been knighted by the King as Knights of the Realm because of their contributions to scientific knowledge. What I want you to see is that a man must have contributed something of unusual value to the Empire in order to be knighted. Both men were great men, great as men speak of worldly greatness; great men intellectually; great men in the secrets of science.

Lake first honored those he met with. He then regaled them with several supernatural stories, as Lake's ministry was filled with supernatural healings and miracles. As they listened, they were stunned and replied:

> Mr. Lake, that is the most wonderful thing we have ever heard. That is the best case of spiritualism we know of. If you will just give us the privilege of publishing that story.

As I have already mentioned, the founders of spiritualism grew up in a form of Christianity that did not operate in the supernatural.

Yet when these spiritualist leaders encountered John G. Lake, they became hungry for what he was experiencing (just like Simon the Sorcerer in Acts 8). The reason many New Agers left the Church in the first place was because the Church is not moving in the supernatural as it is supposed to! To these men, Lake replied:

> Now let me review a moment. Spiritualism is trying to drag the dead up to you. Christianity, bless God, is making the blood-washed spirit go free to the Lord. They are just as opposite as night and day.

Lake went on to record in his journal regarding this meeting:

> In these days when this stuff is being proclaimed around the world by men like Lodge, Doyle, and others who have been recognized as leaders of thought, naturally people are ready to listen.
>
> Years afterward as I considered these things, and discussed them with a brother, he said, "Lake, you had a wonderful opportunity. Tell me, what was the effect in your own soul of that night that you spent with these men?"
>
> I said, "Brother, I left there next morning with profound sympathy in my heart. I said as I walked away, 'Dear God, here are the greatest intellects in the world, but concerning the things of God and the light of the Spirit they are just as blind as though their eyes were sealed.'"

He later wrote:

> One other thing, Conan Doyle is greatly distressed about President Coolidge, and he thinks the proper thing to do is to immediately confer with the spirit of the late President Harding and be directed about the things of

state, or he will make some blunder. This is advice of one of the greatest scientists of all the world, a man who has been knighted by the King of England because of his knowledge of scientific methods. [He is a] bright mind filled with knowledge of this world but a darkened soul without a knowledge of eternal things.[12]

EDGAR EVANS CAYCE (1877–1945)

Edgar Cayce, also known as the "sleeping prophet," was famous for the trance state he would go into while giving revelations. As a child, he aspired to become a missionary and was raised as a member of the Disciples of Christ denomination. He was very devout and claimed to read through the whole Bible every year. From a young age, he experienced strange supernatural phenomena, but a turning point happened when he was thirteen. A woman appeared to him in the spirit and offered to grant him any request. Edgar responded that he wanted to help people when they were sick, especially children.

Later in life, he developed an ability to give people psychic advice regarding their illnesses, which led to many cures. Also, while still young, he had the supernatural ability to sleep with a book under his pillow and awake the next morning with the contents photographically imprinted in his mind.

I was fascinated to read that as a young man Cayce met the famous evangelist D.L. Moody. Moody was traveling through Cayce's town, and Edgar shared with him about the visions and voices he heard. Moody then warned him possession by an evil spirit could create such things. However, according to Cayce's official biography, *There is a River*, the evangelist also left open the possibility that Edgar might be a prophet as described in Numbers 12:6, "Listen to my words: 'When there is a prophet among you, I, the LORD, reveal myself to them in visions, I speak to them in dreams.'"[13] I believe Cayce's calling was to be a prophet according to Numbers 12:6, but he walked off into some serious error. In fact, many regard Cayce as the father of the New Age movement. In my studies, I have come to understand him as the bridge between the old guard (Swedenborg and the Fox Sisters) and the newer developments of the movement.[14]

Although it would be interesting, I will not here go into further depth regarding the New Age movement in the last one hundred years. Especially since the 1960s, Transcendental Meditation and other Eastern Mystical influences have created a vast array of New Age splinter groups and expressions. These make the last one hundred years much more difficult to describe briefly.

As the bridge between the old and the new, Cayce was very much a pioneer in advancing the movement forward, yet at the same time, he was personally impacted by the teachings of Helena Blavatsky and the Theosophy movement, the writings of Swedenborg, and the experiences of Andrew Jackson Davis. John DeSalvo writes in his biography of Davis:

> Did Edgar Cayce know of Andrew Jackson Davis? It appears that Edgar Cayce and his son Hugh Lynn did hear about and were interested in Andrew Jackson Davis. Thomas Sugrue, in his excellent biography of Edgar Cayce, tells this story. Edgar was fishing and Hugh Lynn came to him carrying an old and battered book and said, "This may help us with the scientists. It's a book I've been trying to get for a long time. Someone told me about it. It's the story of a man who lived in this country and did exactly the thing you do, less than a hundred years ago."
>
> Edgar took the book and read the title page: "The Principles of Nature…by Andrew Jackson Davis." As Edgar was reading the book, he said to Hugh Lynn, "This sounds so much like me it gives me the creeps."[15]

Some Simple Conclusions

While many others (Madame Blavatsky, Jeanne Dixon, Shirley MacLaine, Sylvia Brown, and so forth) whom I could mention have been influential in the last one hundred years, I will stop here. As we have observed, the root of the New Age movement began with a theologian who wanted to impact and reform the Church toward the supernatural (Swedenborg). He was followed by a scientist who believed there was more to the universe than the physical world (Mesmer). Then another, with no religious or scientific grid, began to have spiritual revelations and simply recorded them (Davis). Afterward, a small Methodist family had experiences that launched the spiritualist movement (the Fox sisters). A Catholic child became the brilliant Sir Arthur Conan Doyle, who propagated the spiritualist movement far and wide with his writings and reputation. Lastly, a Disciples of Christ member (Cayce) began to fall into trance-like states and give out advice and revelations.

Here are my simple conclusions. I believe, if the Church had been willing to embrace the supernatural and walk with Swedenborg, he would have been able to test his experiences and find some to be false and some to be legitimate. He would have been able to walk in accountability and relationship, to use his gifts inside a spiritual family while walking alongside fellow believers. Instead, because the Church was not healthy and was not operating in the supernatural, he splintered off into his own movement and fell into a lot of weird teachings. It wasn't just Swedenborg, either. This basic pattern is at the root of each of these individuals' stories. Over and over again, gifted people felt they needed to leave the Church to find the supernatural. This leads me to a few questions.

- When such people leave Christianity behind, how do they test their revelations?
- Are they learning from darkness or from light?

- Are they learning and growing, or are they being deceived?

These are not popular questions, but they must be asked. We must determine how one stays on the path of truth and avoids becoming deceived. I will discuss these topics more in the next chapter.

Christian Witchcraft?

Here's what I get from this. If the Church was walking in the supernatural like Jesus did (and like He told us to), there would be no New Age movement. Considering that each of the founders of the New Age movement began in the Church and left when they felt ostracized for operating in the supernatural, we need to reconsider our attitude toward the supernatural.

Many Christian leaders want revival but shy away from the supernatural. Most often this is because the supernatural is difficult to pastor. Considering all the new and unexpected problems that can arise, this is not unreasonable. It will take a generation of brave pastors to reestablish the supernatural as natural for Christians.

It is a risk, but it's one we must take. If we don't embrace the supernatural, we run the even greater risk of alienating young Christians who are beginning to operate in the supernatural and need our guidance. This leads to more and more broken and hurting individuals who reject Jesus because of the wrong actions of His Church. Ultimately, this causes more cults and splinter groups to form—a tragedy that is one hundred percent preventable.

The most recent movement of young people leaving the Church to look for supernatural experience is happening among those who have left powerless Christianity in favor of Wicca and Paganism. These groups go by names such as Christian Wicca and Christopaganism. Their goal is to blend Christianity with nature-based religions.

Nancy Chandler Pittman, author of *Christian Wicca: The Trinitarian Tradition*, writes:

> Why are today's youth looking for spiritual peace and balance in non-Christian based religions? It is simple; the Modern Church in any form or denomination is not doing its job!
>
> This should be a warning sign to all of Christianity! Alarms should be going off to the Modern Church, telling the Church leaders that something is dreadfully wrong in their organizations' spirituality departments. The Modern Organized Christian Churches are letting their young people down, as a direct result, people are looking for spiritual wholeness in the earth-based religions.[16]

Did you read that? "Alarms should be going off to the Modern Church." I don't know about you, but I have been hearing these alarm bells for over a decade. We must change! The onus is on us to become supernatural. Our very relevance is at stake.

Chapter 2

Authentic Versus Counterfeit

...But as his anointing teaches you about all things...that anointing is real, not counterfeit... (1 John 2:27).

As I wrote in the previous chapter, after studying the historic roots of the New Age Movement, I concluded that if the Church had been willing to embrace the supernatural and walk with Swedenborg, he would have been able to test his experiences and find some to be false and some to be legitimate. He would have been able to walk in accountability and relationship, to use his gifts inside a spiritual family while walking alongside fellow believers. He would have been able to discover the difference between authentic supernatural power and the counterfeit.

Counterfeits

Throughout the Bible, we see that everything satan does is a mere counterfeit of an aspect of God's Kingdom. The apostle Paul called these counterfeits "masquerades":

> *And no wonder, for Satan himself **masquerades** as an angel of light. It is not surprising, then, if his servants **masquerade** as servants of righteousness. Their end will be what their actions deserve* (2 Corinthians 11:14–15).

The devil is not a creative being; he operates his kingdom by masquerading as light. To *masquerade* means "to have an appearance that is a mere disguise." In fact, if we studied the nature of the devil throughout the Bible, we would find that the only thing he can do is take something God has created and distort it into something different, making it worse than it was originally meant to be. The nature of the thief's work is to steal, kill, and destroy (see John 10:10).

If the devil only counterfeits, he must first steal everything he does. Thus, for every counterfeit there exists an authentic, which has been replicated. *If there is a counterfeit, there is an authentic that we need to find and reclaim.* Every time we see a masquerade, we need to look closely to properly discern what is being counterfeited, because a counterfeit is evidence that an authentic exists.

Consider the example of counterfeit money. If there is counterfeit money, it proves the existence of real, authentic money. Yet the existence of counterfeit money does not cause us to burn all our real money in order to avoid deception. Instead, we learn to discern between the two. The same is true in the spiritual realm. The existence of counterfeit spiritual power is not reason to shun all spiritual power altogether. Rather, the best response is to pursue the authentic while being aware of the deceptive counterfeit.

For many New Agers, "all that glitters is gold." Yet this is not true. Light and darkness both exist. The truth and lies are realities we must not ignore. Thus, it is very important, while we pursue light and truth and the authentic, to be aware that counterfeits exist and are harmful. We must, as the Bible tells us, *"Examine everything carefully; hold fast to that which is good"* (1 Thess. 5:21 NASB). Each spiritual practice must be tested, and if it is found to be a counterfeit, we must reject it and pursue the authentic instead.

This leads us to the question: *How do we test to see if something is counterfeit?*

The Source

The test to determine whether something is counterfeit or authentic is important, because the wrong testing method can lead us to the wrong conclusion.

To test all counterfeits, both natural and spiritual, we must determine the source. A real Rembrandt painting is authentic because Rembrandt painted it. With counterfeit currency, the question is, "Did this bill originate from the official government mint?" It does not matter whether the counterfeit money or painting looks similar to the original. The counterfeit was created with that precise intent; the best counterfeits look as close to the original as possible, and it is difficult to tell the difference. The test of authenticity is always about origin. This is true of money, paintings, and the spirit realm.

In the spirit realm, the origin of the authentic is God. The way God moves in power looks a lot like the New Age, and this has scared many Christians away from operating in the gifts of the Holy Spirit. Yet it is natural for the authentic supernatural power of the Holy Spirit to look like the counterfeit. Otherwise, satan's power could hardly be called a counterfeit. The very definition involves a close similarity between the two. The best counterfeits closely resemble the real thing they are made to imitate. The counterfeit and the authentic will always look incredibly similar; thus, the main test is the origin.

We find this point powerfully illustrated in the case of Aaron and Moses having a confrontation with Pharaoh's magicians.

> The LORD said to Moses and Aaron, "When Pharaoh says to you, 'Perform a miracle,' then say to Aaron, 'Take your staff and throw it down before Pharaoh,' and it will become a snake" (Exodus 7:8–9).

At that time in history, magicians were well-known for turning their staffs into snakes. It is reasonable to wonder whether Moses and Aaron were concerned how this miracle would make them look to their fellow Hebrews. This would be similar to God telling a local pastor to perform a miracle in the same way the New Age or occult are known for performing miracles. If this scenario took place nowadays, I can imagine at least three reactions from Christians:

1. Some would accuse Moses and Aaron of operating in evil supernatural power, like the religious leaders did to Jesus when He performed deliverance (see Luke 11:14–20).

2. Others would caution Moses and Aaron not to perform this miracle because it would look just like the sorcerers, and they could fall into deception.

3. Some would question whether God even talked to Moses, reasoning that surely God would not tell him to do something the magicians do.

Yet that's exactly what God did. The story continues in this way:

> So Moses and Aaron went to Pharaoh and did just as the LORD commanded. Aaron threw his staff down in front of Pharaoh and his officials and it became a snake. Pharaoh then summoned wise men and sorcerers and the Egyptian magicians also did the same things by their secret arts: Each one threw down his staff and it became a snake. **But Aaron's staff swallowed up their staffs** (Exodus 7:10–12).

If God is our source, we will always defeat the counterfeits. The sorcerers performed an identical miracle; the only difference was the source. Moses was sent from God. The sorcerers operated by "secret [occult] arts." We should not be afraid because the counterfeit and the authentic look the same or worry what others will say about us. If God is the source of our actions, the other powers will always be defeated.

We need to be much more concerned about reclaiming the authentic. We must be more aware of Paul's admonition that we should *not be ignorant of spiritual gifts* (see 1 Cor. 12:1) and that, instead of fearing them, we should *strongly desire* the spiritual gifts (see 1 Cor. 14:1). These verses require more attention in the modern Church if we are going to reclaim everything the enemy has counterfeited.

The Test

One reason it has become increasingly difficult to discern the counterfeit from the authentic is the trend within the New Age movement, over the last few decades, of adopting Christian language. They honor Jesus as a good prophet, claim to interact with the "white light" of the Holy Spirit, and speak of God as their Father. This can confuse a Christian who does not recognize the subtle but important differences between their language and the truth of God's Word. As I have already stated, the main difference between a counterfeit and the authentic is the source; now I will be even more specific about how to discern between the two.

The test of what power source a person is operating in can be boiled down to the question, "Is Jesus the Lord of this person's life?" According to Romans 10:9–10, a person must acknowledge Jesus was raised from the dead and Jesus is the Lord of his or her life. If a person will not agree with these two things, it is a fact that he or she is operating from a source other than the true Jesus of the Bible.

Spiritual practitioners who access and operate in the spirit without Jesus as the Lord of their lives are trespassers in the spirit realm. Jesus put it this way. *"I tell you the truth, the man who does not enter the sheep pen by the gate, but climbs in by some other way, is a thief and a robber"* (John 10:1). Here we find the answer to the common question, "Are psychics and New Agers operating in real power?" The answer is yes, but they have climbed in as trespassers. They have not accessed the spirit realm through Jesus.

God the Father is the Lord of Heaven and earth, and therefore, all realms are His (see Matt. 11:25). There is only one way to be in right relationship to the Father, and that is through His Son, Jesus (see John 14:6). It is Jesus who came to bring us into correct relationship with the Father, and open the heavens—including all the spirit realms—to us (see John 1:15; Matt.16:19; Eph. 2:1-7; Col. 3:1-3). It is the authority of Jesus that protects us from the evil spiritual beings that dwell in the unseen realms.

Without receiving the death, resurrection, and forgiveness of Jesus, we are not in right relationship with the Father. Without right relationship, we are trespassing when we enter into spiritual experiences, and we can be easily deceived and destroyed. It is *dangerous* to operate in spiritual realms without being in right relationship with the Lord of Heaven and earth. We must go into the sheepfold through *the gate*, which is Jesus Christ.

Many people claim Jesus in their spiritual practices but have not actually submitted themselves to His lordship. I believe these are the people Jesus was speaking of when He said:

> *Not everyone who says to Me, "Lord, Lord," will enter the kingdom of heaven, but only he who does the will of my Father who is in heaven. Many will say to Me on that day, "Lord, Lord, did we not prophesy in Your name, and in Your name drive out demons and perform many*

miracles?" Then I will tell them plainly, "I never knew you. Away from me, you evildoers" (Matthew 7:21–23).

Unfortunately, many Christians have beaten themselves up wondering if they are the ones whom Jesus was referring to in this passage. The truth is this group is comprised of people who use Jesus' name but have no personal, experiential relationship with Him. This passage refers to those in the New Age and similar movements who use Christian language but have not submitted to Jesus as their Lord.

Resistance

As we have seen so far, many people operate in the supernatural; some do so safely under the lordship of Jesus Christ, and some (such as Buddhists, Hindus, New Agers, and Occultists) do so dangerously as trespassers.

For those who are reclaiming the authentic supernatural, the greatest resistance actually does not come from those who are walking in the counterfeit but rather from a third group. In the religious world, there are three perspectives on the operation of the supernatural:

1. Those walking in the authentic
2. Those walking in the counterfeit
3. Those walking in neither and afraid of both

Interestingly, group 1 (Christians operating in the power of the Holy Spirit) typically receives the most opposition—not from group 2 (false religionists operating out of evil power sources)—but actually from group 3 (fellow Christians who believe false doctrines regarding the operation of supernatural power). The counterfeit and the authentic look so similar that group 3 frequently declares group 1 is walking in the counterfeit. This is similar to what the Pharisees said of Jesus.

One day Jesus cast out a demon from a man who couldn't speak, and when the demon was gone, the man began to speak. The crowds were amazed, but some of them said, "No wonder he can cast out demons. He gets his power from Satan, the prince of demons (Luke 11:14–15 NLT).

Like the Pharisees, the modern religious spirit does not understand that the existence of the false proves the existence of the authentic. Instead of asking God for discernment to tell the difference, the Pharisees determined, "If they look the same, they are the same."

Considering that even Jesus Himself was accused of walking in dark, supernatural power, we should be prepared for the same accusation. As we reclaim our God-given gifts, we will encounter those who accuse us of falling prey to the counterfeit. A theological failing prevents them from seeing the truth. According to their own theology, all supernatural manifestations in this day and age are counterfeit. Everything supernatural is declared to be a lying sign and wonder. Because of foolish doctrines like Cessationism (the false doctrine that miracles stopped after the supposed "age of the apostles"), much of Western Christianity has abandoned the authentic power of God.

A crafty strategy is often employed by the religious to protect their own doctrines. They will compare a certain branch of the Church with the world, and by drawing parallels, they instill fear and division in the Body of Christ. For example, I have heard it said, "Since the false religion of Mormonism believes in speaking in tongues, it must be of the devil; therefore, when charismatics are speaking in tongues, they must be in collusion with the devil."

Unfortunately, because we have allowed the religious to have such a major influence in the Church, we have driven many young prophets (such as Swedenborg and the rest) away from the Church rather than inviting them to be corrected and mentored by the Church! Surely

God had a calling upon their lives, but because the Church rejected them, they were easily picked off by the enemy. Because they had no grid for testing their revelations, they were easily deceived.

One of the main accusations from the quagmire of religion is that the authentic looks too much like the counterfeit. Considering that the purpose of a counterfeit is to imitate, this accusation is absurd. Their convoluted logic only exposes their fear of the darkness. We were not meant to fear evil but to overcome it with good (see Rom. 12:21). Though religious Christians often resist the Holy Spirit, nonbelievers are more likely to be intrigued and possibly converted by demonstrations of supernatural power. For example, consider how Simon the Sorcerer responded to Peter (see Acts 8). Simon was willing to pay money to have the power of the Holy Spirit! In this reality, we can see the importance of reclaiming the authentic supernatural.

THE COMMISSION

For this reason, we need to begin to use counterfeits as signposts. Every time a counterfeit shows up, we must *take it as the Lord presenting us with an opportunity to reclaim the authentic from the darkness.* Take up the cause to reclaim the Church's stolen property. In the Old Testament, we are told that when a thief is caught he must repay double what he stole (see Exod. 22:3–17). A time is coming when we, the entire Church, will realize we have been robbed of our supernatural goods, and we will confront the thief. When we catch the thief (satan), he will come face-to-face with the fact that he has launched us into double the spirituality and power we had before he robbed us. Retribution day is coming. We just have to identify the counterfeits and reclaim our stuff.

The best way to do this is to become an expert in the authentic. When we see a counterfeit, we don't need to shrink back in fear. Rather, let this cry rise in our hearts— *"That is mine! And I want it back!"*

To start us on this journey, in Part Two of this book, I will analyze sixty-eight spiritual counterfeits and the corresponding authentic, as demonstrated in the Bible. Before I get to that, I will cover one more topic: What happens when the counterfeit and authentic come into direct, open conflict? Such conflicts, which are called power encounters, are the topic of the next two chapters.

Chapter 3

Power Encounters and the Old Testament

The nature of the Kingdom of God is progressive; it is always moving forward and establishing ground for the Lord (see Isa. 9:7). For this reason, I believe the Lord is calling for an increase of power encounters in the days ahead. A *power encounter* is a specific event in which a representative of God comes into open conflict with a representative of a false god. At the end, there is always a clear winner and an equally clear loser. Typically, the winner is able to sway the spectators to follow after his or her God. As the renowned missiologist C. Peter Wagner says,

> A power encounter is a practical, visible demonstration that the power of God is greater than the power of the spirits worshiped or feared by the members of a given social group or by individuals.[1]

Thus we can see that the terms *spiritual warfare* and *power encounter* are not interchangeable. As part of every power encounter, spiritual warfare occurs. However, one can engage in spiritual warfare (even daily) without a power encounter happening. Spiritual warfare is multi-dimensional, including warfare against the flesh, the world system, religious strongholds, political strongholds, and evil supernatural power. At times this includes power encounters, but a power encounter is not implied when spiritual warfare is mentioned.

When we refer to a power encounter, then, we are referring to only one specific experience. This is an important clarification because some people have reduced the term *power encounter* to mean any of the following:

- A powerful experience with the Holy Spirit
- Warfare with territorial principalities
- A powerful deliverance from the demonic
- Angelic warfare, such as Michael struggling with satan in the Book of Jude.

None of these fits the true definition of *power encounter.* Fortunately, the Bible gives us some very clear examples of power encounters—four in the Old Testament and four in the New Testament. From these, we can learn what a power encounter entails and how it applies to our lives. We will look at these in detail in this chapter and the next.

This is important for the days ahead, when power encounters will become more common. The reality is, most Christians are completely unprepared to face off against a representative of evil. This is why, before this increase of power encounters reaches full force, the Lord has placed it on my heart to lay a biblical foundation for this movement. Thus, one of my goals in this book is to prepare Christians for the increase in power encounters between the Body of Christ and many false religions, including Satanism, Wicca, Witchcraft, Mormonism,

Islam, Hinduism, Free Masonry, Buddhism, and the New Age. Here is one key verse that summarizes the purpose and value of power encounters.

> *...to open their eyes and turn them from darkness to light, and from the power of Satan to God, so that they may receive forgiveness of sins and a place among those who are sanctified by faith in me* (Acts 26:18).

Understanding God's Heart

As Acts 26:18 makes clear, the purpose of power encounters is always to win people over to the heart of God. Unfortunately, many Christians have misunderstood the heart of God, and those who misunderstand His heart end up misrepresenting Him to others. In all things, we must understand the motivations of God's heart and make sure our motivations align with His.

In the light of God's love, we must take a fresh look at God's heart toward those who are representatives of false gods. Otherwise, we will never be able to represent Him correctly in a power encounter.

Fortunately for us, in the Old Testament, God communicated very clearly His position toward those who operate under the power of false gods, giving four progressive warnings and declarations that demonstrate how He feels about people who use evil power.

1. Defilement

> First, God declared that operating with evil power sources would defile His people. *"Do not turn to mediums or seek out spiritists, for **you will be defiled by them**. I am the LORD your God"* (Lev. 19:31).

2. Prohibition

Second, because God wanted to protect His people from defilement, He prohibited them from engaging with demonic power.

> *When you enter the land the LORD your God is giving you, do not learn to imitate the detestable ways of the nations there. Let no one be found among you who sacrifices his son or daughter in the fire, who practices divination or sorcery, interprets omens, engages in witchcraft, or casts spells, or who is a medium or spiritist or who consults the dead. Anyone who does these things is detestable to the LORD, and because of these detestable practices the LORD your God will drive out those nations before you. You must be blameless before the LORD your God* (Deuteronomy 18:9–13).

3. Separation

Third, to show the importance of obedience, God had to enforce His prohibition. For those who decided to persist in disobedience and chose to be defiled by satan's power, God created consequences. Deliverance did not exist in the Old Testament. The choice to give oneself over to evil was permanent. Thus, when people gave themselves over to evil supernatural power, God had to separate them from His people for their protection. The Old Testament laws were always intended to protect God's people from being entrapped by the destructive power of false gods.

> *I will set my face against the person who turns to mediums and spiritists to prostitute himself by following them, and I will cut him off from his people* (Leviticus 20:6).

4. Death Penalty

In the previous three statements we find a progression: First, God declares they will be defiled; second, He tells His people to stay away; and third, He says His people must separate themselves from anyone who seeks out the defiling practices. Here, in the fourth statement, we find what happens when a person has actually chosen to become a medium or spiritist. In that case, that person has passed the first three statements and must be put to death to keep such practices from spreading through the nation.

The death penalty was the ultimate consequence. We must keep in mind that this was the last and final way to address the issue. God extended the first three declarations as warnings about evil supernatural power and gave time and opportunity for repentance. Ultimately, the death penalty was the final resort to protect God's people from defilement. *"A man or woman who is a medium or spiritist among you must be put to death. You are to stone them; their blood will be on their own heads"* (Lev. 20:27).

Many Christians have misrepresented God's heart by going straight to the fourth declaration and claiming God desires to kill all witches and warlocks. A more accurate understanding is this: God wanted to protect His people from destructive spiritual forces. He started by setting up a prohibition; then to help His people understand the seriousness of this danger, He even put consequences in place. Lastly, to strike fear into the hearts of the disobedient, He gave the death penalty as the ultimatum.

God did not desire to kill sorcerers, magicians, warlocks, witches, and astrologers; God wanted to protect His people, and He wanted them to clearly understand the danger of these evils. As we will see later, when Daniel had a power encounter, and the king was going to kill all the magicians, Daniel, as God's representative, told the king not to kill them. Even in the Old Testament, God loved all people and wanted to redeem them from evil supernatural power. If we believe the God of the Bible just wants to kill witches, we will be contradicting Him if we love them. But if we understand His true heart toward them, we will be free to respond to them in love. That is why it is important to understand that God loves all people and that His goal with the Old Testament Law was to warn and protect people from evil.

Old Testament Power Encounters

With the framework of a loving God firmly established, now let's look in-depth at four individuals in the Old Testament who engaged in power encounters. (In the next chapter, we will look at four from the New Testament.) With each of these individuals, we will see how God prepared them beforehand. Each of these individuals had the potential to impact anywhere from hundreds to many millions of lives depending on their ability to win the power encounter. With so much at risk, God was willing to take many years to prepare them for the battles of their lives.

For example, Moses had the nation of Israel depending on him for their freedom and ability to escape Egypt. If Moses had lost, how would the story have ended? Joseph had to interpret a dream correctly or a massive famine would have killed hundreds of thousands of people. Daniel had to interpret a dream correctly or the king would have killed him, his fellow Hebrew captives, and all the wise men in the country (perhaps hundreds or thousands of people's lives were at stake). Elijah had the soul of the nation of Israel at stake when he had to battle the 850 evil prophets on Mount Carmel. Very few in history have ever had to face power encounters of this magnitude. The power encounters we may have to engage in may pale in comparison to these Old Testament stories. But because of the great detail in these stories, we can glean many insights from a closer look.

One of the most comforting of these insights is that each of these four individuals had years of training before the Lord gave them such a heavy responsibility. Moses spent forty years learning how to herd sheep in the wilderness before God put him in the place of herding the Israelites for forty years in the wilderness. Joseph had to endure seventeen years of being disgraced, mistreated, and lied about in order to prepare him for handling the favor and honor of being made the second in command over all Egypt. Daniel stood up against the peer pressure to conform, and then, when his power encounter came, he was able to literally save the lives of those who had been pressuring him to conform. Elijah was treated as an outcast of society. He was blamed for the national draught (rather than the nation seeing that the draught was because of their sin), and he felt like he was the only one still faithful to the Lord. Elijah did not even have a traveling companion or apprentice until the Lord gave him one. Yet even as an outcast, Elijah devoted his life to turning the heart of the nation back to God. The Lord taught Elijah to love the very nation that was rejecting him.

As we look at each of these stories in more depth, we will ask four main questions of each power encounter in Scripture:

1. Who initiated the power encounter?
2. Where is the heart of God in the encounter?
3. Who won the encounter?
4. What happened as a result of winning the encounter?

As we examine each encounter through the lens of these questions, many insights will be gained. We will find that some of the questions have consistent answers, whereas some have varied answers. This is important, because Scripture sets the precedent for what we should expect in our own experiences.

CASE ONE: JOSEPH VS. PHARAOH'S MAGICIANS
(GENESIS 41)

When the Pharaoh of Egypt had a very troubling dream, he called for his magicians to interpret it. Perhaps in the past his magicians had given him some good interpretations, but this time none of them had anything to say. That was when Pharaoh's cupbearer remembered that, while he was in prison, Joseph had given him a detailed and accurate interpretation of his dream. The cupbearer suggested Pharaoh call Joseph from the prison.

When Joseph appeared before Pharaoh, he was very humble about his ability to interpret dreams. Rather than touting his own ability, he declared that God was the one who would give the interpretation of the dream. And of course He did. After Joseph gave the accurate interpretation of the dream, Pharaoh poured favor on Joseph, placing him as the second-in-command over all of Egypt. (For the full story of Joseph's life, read Genesis 37–47.)

1. *Who initiated the power encounter?* God initiated and coordinated this power encounter.

2. *Where is the heart of God in the encounter?* God intentionally saved Egypt (Joseph included) from the coming famine.

3. *Who won the encounter?* Joseph emerged as the victor and was promoted from the prison to the palace.

4. *What happened as a result of winning the encounter?* The nation was saved from famine, Joseph's extended family found favor in Egypt, and God was glorified.

I want to highlight a few interesting points in this passage. First, Joseph went through years of preparation for his moment before

Pharaoh. He was abused by his brothers, sold into slavery, lied about, thrown into prison, and forgotten. Clearly he had a lot of opportunities to become offended at his family, his masters, his cellmates, and his God. Fortunately, he chose to extend forgiveness instead. The Lord spent approximately seventeen years preparing Joseph before the visions of his youth came to pass.

Second, it is also interesting to note that Joseph did not have any ability to initiate this power encounter. He was still sitting in prison, just like any other day, when suddenly the guard came to tell him Pharaoh wanted to see him. After all that time, Joseph must have been a little startled.

Third, God's heart in this power encounter was to show that even an outcast sitting in the bottom of the prison who had a real relationship with God could triumph over the professionally trained magicians of Pharaoh's court. This must have been a painful scene for the magicians to watch, but God had prepared his man for years, and Joseph was able to save millions of people (including the magicians) from starving to death.

Case Two: Moses vs. the Egyptian Magicians (Exodus 7–11)

In this case, God also initiated the power encounter, telling Moses exactly what to do and say. God even told Moses in advance how Pharaoh would respond. Interestingly, God told Moses Pharaoh would demand the performance of a miracle. In response to Pharaoh's demand, God said Moses should have Aaron throw down his staff and it would become a snake. Pharaoh's magicians were able to reproduce this first miracle, but even in that, Aaron's staff/snake ate up the magicians' staffs/snakes. This was the first step in proving Moses' and Aaron's superiority.

God went on to perform ten supernatural plagues in Egypt through Moses. It is fascinating to watch the progressive response of Pharaoh's magicians. They were able to reproduce the staff turning into a snake; they also were able to reproduce the first two plagues: the water turning to blood and the frogs. When the third plague occurred (that of the gnats), the magicians were unable to reproduce it. From the third plague onward, the magicians could not reproduce any more of Moses' plagues. Out of ten plagues, Pharaoh's magicians could only reproduce the first two.

When the magician's failed at plague three, they proclaimed about Moses, *"This is the finger of God"* (Exod. 8:19). The plague of boils (the sixth plague) actually afflicted the magicians so badly they could not even appear before Moses. By the time of the eighth plague (the locusts), Pharaoh's officials were saying, *"How long will this man be a snare to us? Let the people go, so that they may worship the LORD their God. Do you not yet realize that Egypt is ruined?"* (Exod. 10:7). Finally, when the tenth plague was killing the firstborns of Egypt, Moses said of Pharaoh's officials, *"All these officials of yours will come to me, bowing down before me and saying, 'Go, you and all the people who follow you'"* (Exod. 11:8). Moses so thoroughly won this series of power encounters that the magicians wanted Moses to leave the country.

1. *Who initiated the power encounter?* God sent a very resistant Moses to encounter Pharaoh.

2. *Where is the heart of God in the encounter?* God extended many opportunities for Pharaoh to let the Israelites go peacefully. God's heart was to see His people set free.

3. *Who won the encounter?* Moses dominated the power encounter from start to finish.

4. *What happened as a result of winning the encounter?*

The Israelites went free, and in the process, Pharaoh's magicians recognized the God of Moses trumps them completely.

God's desire was to bring His people out of Egypt to bless them and give them their own country. Joseph had brought them to Egypt centuries earlier to give them food during the famine and the safety of his rulership. As the years progressed, the memory of Joseph faded from the culture, and the Israelites were seen as a possible threat to the Egyptians. As a result, they were forced into hard labor and even required to kill their own children to control the population. At that point, God began to intervene by providing a Moses.

God had Moses trained in the house of Pharaoh yet gave him a heart for his brothers, the Israelites. Then God sent him to the wilderness for forty years, where he herded sheep, in order to prepare him physically, mentally, and emotionally for the forty-year trek in the wilderness he would lead three million Israelites on.

Case Three: Daniel vs. the Babylonian Wise Men (Daniel 1–5)

Daniel is one of the most extraordinary individuals in the Bible, one of the reasons being that he was engaged in three unique power encounters. Truly, his story is one of my favorites to read. Daniel was a Hebrew captive in Babylon who had been chosen for special training in Babylonian culture. Daniel was highly educated in the natural areas of literature as well as supernaturally gifted in understanding visions and dreams of all kinds. The king even said he had found none equal to Daniel, that in *every area* of wisdom and understanding, Daniel was ten times better than all the magicians and enchanters in his kingdom (see Dan. 1:17–20).

Power Encounter #1 (Daniel 2)

Daniel's first power encounter occurred when King Nebuchadnezzar had a dream that needed interpreting. The king called for his astrologers and commanded them to give him the interpretation, but he refused to tell the astrologers what the dream was. Thus they received the difficult task of telling the king what the dream was, without natural knowledge, and then giving an accurate interpretation. To add to the stress of this difficult task, the king gave an ultimatum, threatening to cut them to pieces and destroy their houses if they didn't tell him both the dream and the interpretation correctly.

The astrologers told the king it was impossible, that no man could do what he demanded. But the king was immovable in his decision, and he began to gather all the magicians and astrologers, including Daniel, to put them to death. When Daniel heard of it, he asked for time to seek God for the answer to the king's request.

I find it interesting that Daniel asked the king not to put all the astrologers and magicians to death. Then he gave God all the credit for the dream and interpretation. Lastly, he gave the king a perfect rendering of the dream with the full interpretation. In response, the king promoted Daniel to chief of the magicians. Rather than Daniel having all of his opponents put to death, he chose to rule over them. (I believe this is similar to the Church's interaction with satan; rather than destroying satan, God gave us the ability to triumph in Christ, and then He put the Church here to subdue the power of satan.)

Power Encounter #2 (Daniel 4:4–9)

By the time Daniel's second power encounter occurred, he was already well established as the chief of the magicians. The king was once again having troubling dreams and needed interpretations. He started by calling the lower level magicians, and again they failed to bring the interpretation of his dreams. Finally, Daniel came into the presence of the king. We can tell from what is written that the king had faith in Daniel to be able to give him the interpretation. The king went so far as to say, *"No mystery is too difficult for you"* (Dan. 4:9).

Once again, by the supernatural ability God had given him, Daniel triumphed over the competition. This is a great precedent for the Church. By flowing in the anointing the Lord gives us, we can triumph over all the powers of the enemy.

POWER ENCOUNTER #3 (DANIEL 5:5–31)

By the time of Daniel's third power encounter, King Nebuchadnezzar had died and Daniel's reputation had waned. Nebuchadnezzar's son, Belshazzar, had taken his place as the new king. While he was having a large party, a hand appeared in midair and began to write on the wall. The terrified king called for all his wise men to interpret the words the hand had written. None were able. Finally, the king's wife said,

> *There is a man in your kingdom who has the spirit of the holy gods in him. In the time of your father he was found to have insight and intelligence and wisdom like that of the gods. King Nebuchadnezzar your father—your father the king, I say—appointed him chief of the magicians, enchanters, astrologers and diviners. This man Daniel, whom the king called Belteshazzar, was found to have a keen mind and knowledge and understanding, and also the ability to interpret dreams, explain riddles and solve difficult problems. Call for Daniel, and he will tell you what the writing means* (Daniel 5:11–12).

When summoned, Daniel appeared before the king, and as before, he provided the interpretation. In response, the king made Daniel the third highest ruler in the whole kingdom. This was somewhat in vain, considering the interpretation was actually a word of judgment. That same night, the Medes came, killed Belshazzar, and took over the kingdom.

Let's consider our questions related to all three of Daniel's power encounters.

1. *Who initiated the power encounter?* In all three cases, the king called for Daniel and invited him to give the interpretation.

2. *Where is the heart of God in the encounter?* God was the one speaking to the pagan kings in all three cases, which demonstrates His graciousness. Also, He provided Daniel as His representative to interpret the dreams. By putting Daniel in place, God showed how much He cares to speak, even to pagan kings.

3. *Who won the encounter?* In all three cases, the magicians failed, and Daniel perfectly interpreted the dreams.

4. *What happened as a result of winning the encounters?* Daniel got promoted repeatedly, God was glorified, and the other magicians were put in subjugation.

Daniel lived a life of extraordinary power encounters. Throughout the many accounts in Scripture, no other individual had as many high-level power encounters as Daniel. As we have seen with Joseph and Moses, Daniel also did not initiate the encounters; the king summoned him for an interpretation each time. In fact, in the first power encounter, the king actually put a death penalty over the interpreters' heads.

Following in the footsteps of Joseph and Moses, Daniel also didn't call for the death of the magicians; he had a clear opportunity to do so, but he chose not to kill them. Instead, Daniel was put in charge over them as the chief magician after he put them to shame with his amazing interpretations.

Like both Joseph and Moses, Daniel won the power encounter by triumphing over his competitors' abilities. As Second Corinthians 2:14 says, *"But thanks be to God, who always leads us in triumph in Christ, and manifests through us the sweet aroma of the knowledge of Him in every place"* (NASB).

Case Four: Elijah vs. the Prophets of Baal (1 Kings 18:16–40)

Elijah was a prophet to Israel during the reign of the wicked King Ahab and his wife Jezebel, who had led Israel to abandon God and worship Baal and Asherah (false gods) instead. Elijah was the only remaining prophet of the Lord, and because he spoke openly against Ahab and Jezebel, he was regularly threatened with death. All of this climaxed in a showdown between Elijah and the 450 prophets of Baal and the 400 prophets of Asherah.

Elijah initiated this power encounter by calling Ahab to summon all of his false prophets (as well as all the people of Israel) to meet him on Mount Carmel. When everyone was gathered, Elijah said to them, *"How long will you waver between two opinions? If the LORD is God, follow him; but if Baal is God, follow him"* (1 Kings 18:21). In other words, he challenged the people to choose who their God would be based on the results of the forthcoming power encounter.

Elijah told the people to bring two bulls and allowed the false prophets to have their pick of the two. He then instructed them to slaughter the bull, build an altar, place wood on the altar, and place the pieces of the bull on top of the wood—but not to set fire to it.

Once they finished, Elijah told the false prophets to call on the name of their god to light their sacrifice on fire. This they did from morning till noon with no results. After several hours, Elijah began to taunt them:

> At noon Elijah began to taunt them. "Shout louder!" he said. "Surely he is a god! Perhaps he is deep in thought, or busy, or traveling. Maybe he is sleeping and must be awakened" (1 Kings 18:27).

The false prophets did just that, shouting louder and slashing themselves with swords for several more hours—all in an effort to get a response from their god. Still, nothing happened.

Finally, Elijah called the people to watch him as he repaired the altar of the Lord, which had been in ruins. He then dug a trench around the altar, arranged wood on top of the altar, cut his bull into pieces, and arranged it on the wood. Then Elijah upped the ante by having the people dump four large jugs of water over the sacrifice—three times. The water thoroughly soaked the altar and filled the trench around it. No human could have set that altar on fire. Then Elijah prayed:

> O LORD, God of Abraham, Isaac and Israel, let it be known today that you are God in Israel and that I am your servant and have done all these things at your command. Answer me, O LORD, answer me, so these people will know that you, O LORD, are God, and that you are turning their hearts back again (1 Kings 18:36–37).

Immediately, the fire of the Lord fell from Heaven and burned up the sacrifice, the wood, the stones, the dirt, and even the water in the trench. When the people saw it, they fell to their faces and repented, turning back to the Lord. In response, Elijah commanded the people to seize the false prophets. The people captured all 850 false prophets and killed them in a nearby valley. This was a great victory for God, but when Jezebel heard about it, she began to hunt Elijah in order to put him to death.

1. *Who initiated the power encounter?* Uniquely, Elijah was the instigator of this power encounter.

2. *Where is the heart of God in the encounter?* God was working through His prophet to rebuke His idolatrous people.

3. *Who won the encounter?* Elijah was the victor

4. *What happened as a result of winning the encounter?* Many pagan priests were put to death, and Israel temporary turned back to God. Elijah was not promoted but was instead hunted by Jezebel.

The nature of Elijah's power encounter with the prophets of Baal and Asherah differs greatly from the power encounters we have observed so far. Since this is the most well known and commonly referenced power encounter in Scripture, it is important to notice the differences.

First, this encounter took place within Israel. The other encounters—of Joseph, Moses, and Daniel—happened while these men were captives in foreign countries where Israeli law did not apply. For this reason, the idea of killing their power encounter opponents was not even considered. In the case of Elijah, he was actually cleansing the Israelite land of all the evil King Ahab had allowed by enforcing the Mosaic Law within the borders of Israel's kingdom. He killed 450 prophets of Baal and 400 prophets of Asherah in the first and only power encounter in Scripture where someone was put to death.

Second, in the cases of Joseph and Moses, God had not yet given the Law to the Israelites, so they didn't have the ordinance to kill sorcerers. Daniel did have the Mosaic Law at the time of his encounters, but he was a captive and chose not to impose foreign law on the Babylonians. We see this clearly in the fact that, even when the king created the opportunity to put all the sorcerers to death, Daniel requested he spare their lives.

Third, Elijah initiated the confrontation. None of the other three men we studied initiated their encounters. Moses, against his will, was commanded by the Lord to confront Pharaoh. By contrast, Elijah instigated the challenge of his own accord. Here we see two very different precedents in the Old Testament. The question is, *Which of these Old Testament precedents applies to us today as New Testament believers?* Since many of us are not Hebrews and we are not living in Old Testament Israel under Mosaic Law, which precedent applies to us?

Elijah was confronting sin inside Israel according to Mosaic Law. Many mistaken leaders have tried to use Elijah as an example of how Christians should confront the New Age movement. However, Joseph, Moses, and Daniel provide truer examples of how Christians should interact with practitioners of evil power. Their power encounters depict what we should expect.

I don't believe Elijah's power encounter is a good precedent for New Testament believers. What he did was right for that time and place, but I don't believe his situation applies to us. Rather, in the next chapter, I will develop a cohesive picture of what we should expect in power encounters as New Testament believers.

Chapter 4

Power Encounters and the Church

In the last chapter, we defined the term *power encounter* and analyzed the four primary power encounters in the Old Testament. We also talked about the differences between the power encounters that happened in foreign contexts and Elijah's power encounter within Israel. Now let's look at the power encounters in the New Testament Church to glean even more information on what power encounters should look like for the modern Christian.

New Testament Power Encounters

Case One: The Apostle Peter vs. Simon the Sorcerer (Acts 8:4–25)

The first New Testament power encounter happened between Peter and a sorcerer named Simon, who lived in Samaria and had great influence in the area.

> *He [Simon] boasted that he was someone great, and all the people, both high and low, gave him their attention and exclaimed, "This man is the divine power known as the Great Power." They followed him because he had amazed them for a long time with his magic.*

But when Philip came to Samaria and began preaching the gospel, performing many miracles and casting out evil spirits, the people turned to Christ in great numbers. Even Simon the sorcerer was baptized and followed Philip everywhere, being continually amazed by the signs he performed. When the apostles heard what was happening in Samaria, Peter and John came and prayed for the people to receive the Holy Spirit (whom they had not yet received). When Simon saw that everyone whom they laid hands upon received the Spirit, he approached the apostles, offering them money and saying, *"Give me also this ability so that everyone on whom I lay my hands may receive the Holy Spirit"* (Acts 8:19).

Peter answered him:

> *May your money perish with you, because you thought you could buy the gift of God with money! You have no part or share in this ministry, because your heart is not right before God. Repent of this wickedness and pray to the Lord. Perhaps he will forgive you for having such a thought in your heart. For I see that you are full of bitterness and captive to sin* (Acts 8:20–23).

In the face of Peter's rebuke, Simon did not repent but simply asked the apostles to pray that no calamity would come upon him. That is the last we hear of him.

In summary, Simon was the primary spiritual influence in the region prior to Philip's arrival, and he was astonished by the miracles Philip performed. Because of this, he accepted Philip's teachings and was baptized, yet evil desires and mindsets remained in him, causing him to try to buy the anointing. For this, Peter rebuked him strongly. We do not know for sure how Simon responded to that rebuke.

I appreciate and agree with Peter Wagner's assessment of the story:

> This story contains many unknowns. Was Simon's original profession of faith and baptism valid or just a sham? After Peter later rebuked him, did he repent? As far as Simon the Sorcerer is concerned, does the story have a happy or a sad ending? Although I have no way of proving it, I would like to believe that Simon was really saved through Philip's preaching, that he subsequently made a huge mistake as a new babe in Christ, that the Holy Spirit used Peter's rebuke to straighten him out, and that he repented and lived happily ever after.[1]

Whether this was the case or not, the most important question is, what can we learn from this story? In our culture, it may seem strange to us that Simon offered money for Peter's power, but in that day, it was a common practice among professional magicians and sorcerers to pay one another for the secrets of their power. When Simon saw the much greater power wielded by the apostles, he wanted it too, and he asked for it in the only way he knew.

As Yale University biblical scholar Susan Garrett says of this power encounter:

> Satan does still have some power, but he is handily subjugated when confronted by the vastly greater divine authority that Christians wield. Peter's righteous rebuke reduces Simon from a famous magician, impiously acclaimed by all the people of Samaria as 'the great power of God,' to a meek man who fears for his own destruction and asks the servant of the Lord to intercede for him.[2]

In other words, the story of Simon shows us the significant difference between the powers of darkness and the power of God. Greater than simply showing the contrast, the thing I appreciate most about this story is that it shows the hunger that exists for the authentic power of God. Nonbelievers want the authentic, and when it comes close, they will cry out for it.

Case Two: The Apostle Paul vs. Elymas the Sorcerer (Acts 13:6–12)

In this second story, the apostle Paul encountered a Jewish sorcerer and false prophet named Elymas, who was an attendant to the proconsul in Paphos. Unlike Simon the sorcerer, Elymas was not friendly toward the Christians. When the proconsul sent to Paul and Barnabas so he could hear the word of the Lord, Elymas opposed them and tried to dissuade the proconsul from the gospel. This led Paul, full of the Spirit, to confront Elymas in a dramatic power encounter. Paul looked right at Elymas and said:

> *You are a child of the devil and an enemy of everything that is right! You are full of all kinds of deceit and trickery. Will you never stop perverting the right ways of the Lord? Now the hand of the Lord is against you. You are going to be blind, and for a time you will be unable to see the light of the sun* (Acts 13:10–11).

Immediately, Elymas lost his vision and began groping about for someone to help him. The amazed proconsul, who witnessed the confrontation, immediately believed in the Lord.

This passage gives us textbook clarity for defining a power encounter. Paul was *"filled with the Holy Spirit"* (Acts 13:9) while his opponent, Elymas, was *"full of all deceit and all fraud"* and was a *"son of the devil"* (Acts 13:10). Paul's goal was to persuade the proconsul to believe in the gospel. Elymas, his opponent, was trying to manipulate and control the situation spiritually.

Suddenly, Paul initiated a power encounter by confronting Elymas. Paul called out the evil surrounding Elymas and made a powerful declaration against him that caused him to go blind. This demonstration of the all-powerful Kingdom of God was evidence enough for the proconsul. He was so amazed by the demonstration of power that he turned his life over to Jesus. This is a good example of a New Testament Christian initiating a power encounter. It's important to notice the purpose of the power encounter was to demonstrate the Kingdom to the proconsul, not to convert the sorcerer.

Case Three: The Apostle Paul vs. the Fortune Telling Slave Girl (Acts 16:16–21)

The third power encounter in the Book of Acts involved a slave girl who was possessed by a spirit that enabled her to predict the future. Because of her ability as a fortune teller, her masters were able to make a lot of money. When this girl encountered Paul and Silas, she began following them, shouting *"These men are servants of the Most High God, who are telling you the way to be saved"* (Acts 16:17). She did this for several days until Paul became so troubled by it that he rebuked the spirit and commanded it to come out of the girl. Instantly, it left. The girl's owners, realizing their hope of making money was gone, seized Paul and Silas and took them before the authorities, accusing them of creating an uproar and advocating unlawful customs. As a result, Paul and Silas were beaten and thrown into prison.

It's important to note two points here. First, Paul confronted the spirit, *not* the slave girl, and second, He was not concerned about the impact upon the girl's owners, who were motivated by money and did not care about the girl or her deliverance. Unlike the girl's owners, Paul was concerned for this girl's freedom, and through a power encounter with the spirit that controlled her, he set her free.

Wagner's commentary on this passage provides more detail:

> How was it that they could make so much money through this fortune-teller? The obvious answer is that this slave girl was good at fortune-telling. She knew the future, and she had built a sound reputation for accuracy. The slave girl had not gained her stature in the occult community by making constant mistakes.
>
> The slave girl in Philippi was demonized with a spirit of divination, Acts 16:16. Our English Bible versions translate the Greek *pneuma python* by using the functional name of this spirit, 'spirit of divination' or 'spirit of clairvoyance,' instead of the proper name, 'Python Spirit.'
>
> If Paul had cast out the Python spirit the first day, few probably would have known about it. But when it finally happened, it turned out to be a major public display of the power of God over the power of Satan, and the territorial spirit over Philippi was thoroughly embarrassed.[3]

Unlike in Paul's encounter with the sorcerer Elymas, Paul didn't rebuke the slave girl directly; he rebuked the demonic spirit. What's the difference? Freewill. Elymas chose of his own will to resist Paul. By contrast, the fortune-telling girl was a slave, and she had to obey her masters and submit herself to demonic possession for their gain. I believe she followed them around for days because she could literally see the anointing on them as men of God and she desired freedom in her heart. After several days, Paul discerned the slave girl's desire for freedom, so rather than rebuking her, he rebuked the demon and set her free spiritually.

Case Four: The Seven Sons of Sceva, a Power Encounter Gone Wrong (Acts 19:11–22)

The fourth power encounter in Acts did not go so well. It is a perfect example of what not to do when confronting the powers of darkness. Here's what happened.

Seven Jewish brothers, the seven sons of Sceva, a Jewish chief priest, observed the extraordinary miracles God was doing through Paul. Though they were not believers in Jesus, they decided to mimic Paul's ministry by using the name of Jesus to cast out demons.

> *One day the evil spirit answered them, "Jesus I know, and I know about Paul, but who are you?" Then the man who had the evil spirit jumped on them and overpowered them all. He gave them such a beating that they ran out of the house naked and bleeding* (Acts 19:15–16).

Some unbelievers, like these seven brothers, don't have a relationship with Jesus, but they recognize the power in His name. Obviously, these brothers overstepped their authority, and as a result, they were beaten and humiliated by the demonized man. From this we can learn that the power of Jesus' name functions only through relationship.

Some modern teachers contend that using the name of Jesus and deliverance are all based in the psychological power of suggestion. Such an idea is readily debunked through this story, in which the demon refuses to obey the seven sons of Sceva because of their lack of relationship with Jesus. They didn't have access to the authority of Jesus' name, but the demon-possessed man couldn't have known that in the natural. If it was all just the power of suggestion, the sons of Sceva would have been successful. Instead, the spiritual presence inside the man recognized their lack of true authority (despite their use of Jesus' name), and through demonic power, this one man pulverized all seven wannabe deliverance ministers.

But look at what happened next:

> *When this became known to the Jews and Greeks living in Ephesus, they were all seized with fear, and the name of the Lord Jesus was held in high honor. Many of those who believed now came and openly confessed their evil deeds. A number who had practiced sorcery brought their scrolls together and burned them publicly. When they calculated the value of the scrolls, the total came to fifty thousand drachmas. In this way the word of the Lord spread widely and grew in power* (Acts 19:17–20).

The failure of the seven sons of Sceva proved that only believers have power to access the name of Jesus. Amazingly, this failed power encounter actually turned into a holy fear of the true name of Jesus and resulted in a regional revival.

Case Five: The Early Church vs. Demetrius the Idol-Maker (Acts 19:23–41)

The fifth power encounter recorded in Acts happened when Paul began leading many Ephesians away from idol worship to worship the true God. Because Ephesus was the home of the Greek goddess Artemis, much of the industry there was connected to idol worship. It's not surprising, then, that some of the idol makers began to feel threatened by the conversions to Christianity. As a result:

> *A silversmith named Demetrius, who made silver shrines of Artemis, brought in no little business for the craftsmen. He called them together, along with the workmen in related trades, and said: "Men, you know we receive a good income from this business. And you see and hear how this fellow Paul has convinced and led astray large numbers of people here in Ephesus and in practically the whole province of Asia. He says that man-made gods are*

> *no gods at all. There is danger not only that our trade will lose its good name, but also that the temple of the great goddess Artemis will be discredited, and the goddess herself, who is worshiped throughout the province of Asia and the world, will be robbed of her divine majesty."*
>
> *When they heard this, they were furious and began shouting: "Great is Artemis of the Ephesians!" Soon the whole city was in an uproar...* (Acts 19:24–29).

The angry mob seized several of Paul's companions and took them to the theater, where many people had gathered. There was much shouting and confusion, and most of the people didn't even know why they were there or what the problem was. Though Paul wanted to go to the theater and address the assembly, his friends strongly warned him against it. Eventually, the city clerk quieted the crowd, reprimanding them for making such a disturbance and putting their city in danger of being charged with rioting. Further, he told Demetrius and the other craftsmen to take their grievances to the courts, where they could be settled properly. With that, he sent the crowds home, and the protest ended. (See Acts 19:35–41.)

Technically speaking, this was *almost* a power encounter. We have both sides represented in the story; we even have a crowd to be won. But the battle was never actually engaged. Speculating, based on all the other stories in Scripture, I expect if Paul had come into open conflict with Demetrius, Demetrius would have been readily defeated. Scripture holds no evidence of God's children ever losing a power encounter. In this case, the conflict was dissolved by the natural authorities before a face-off took place.

Conclusion

The New Testament power encounters we have examined fall into three categories. First, we have those in which God's representative is the undisputed winner. Second, we have the sons of Sceva, who were not representatives of God but who tried to battle and were shamefully defeated. Third is the only time when the enemy called for a power encounter, but the battle was never engaged.

In both the Old and New Testament power encounters, we found that God always won and His heart was to free people from their slavish bondage to demonic entities. The same is true in every power encounter. God is not an arrogant show off who needs to trounce the devil to feel like a big God. His real heart is to see those in bondage to demonic forces set free. God is love, and therefore, even when He is demonstrating His fierce power, He still is doing so from a heart flowing in love and freedom.

The Ark of the Covenant vs. the god Dagon

The following Scripture verses tell of an interesting occurrence in Israel's history. It technically does not qualify as a power encounter under the definition we are working with, which is why it was not included in Chapter Three. However, I do find it worthy of mention in our study.

Here is the setting. The Philistines had stolen the Ark of the Covenant (the earthly expression of God's manifest presence) from the Israelites. When the Philistines put the Ark in their temple with the false god Dagon, a sort of power encounter occurred.

> *After the Philistines had captured the ark of God, they took it from Ebenezer to Ashdod. Then they carried the ark into Dagon's temple and set it beside Dagon. When the people of Ashdod rose early the next day, there was Dagon, fallen on his face on the ground before the ark of the LORD! They took Dagon and put him back in his place. But the following morning when they rose, there was Dagon, fallen on his face on the ground before the ark*

of the LORD! His head and hands had been broken off and were lying on the threshold; only his body remained (1 Samuel 5:1–4).

Just the presence of the Ark caused the idol to be defeated. The story continues with the Philistines passing the Ark to several other towns, with judgment falling on each town, until they finally sent the Ark back to Israel.

We Are the Ark

In the New Testament, the believer is the place of the manifest presence of God. The Ark of the Covenant—which contained the Ten Commandments, the rod of Aaron, and manna from the desert—foreshadowed New Testament realities.

1. The Ten Commandments: We as believers have the law of the Lord written on our hearts (see Heb. 10:16).

2. The Rod of Aaron: We carry resurrection life and power within us, which is what Aaron's rod represented.

3. The Manna: We also are partakers of the hidden manna, as Jesus said, *"I am the Bread of life"* (John 6:48).

Paul even called the body of a believer the temple of God.

> *Don't you know that you yourselves are God's temple and that God's Spirit dwells in your midst? If anyone destroys God's temple, God will destroy that person; for God's temple is sacred, and you together are that temple* (1 Corinthians 3:16–17 NIV).

Similarly, a few chapters later, Paul says:

Do you not know that your body is a temple of the Holy Spirit, who is in you, whom you have received from God?
(1 Corinthians 6:19a)

In other words, New Testament believers have been made to be God's temple. We carry the Ark of His presence in our hearts. Thus, the story of Dagon falling before the Ark until it was destroyed is an Old Testament example of the New Testament reality. We as individuals carry the power of God within us, and we should steward it with full awareness of its power and authority. We contain all the power we need to see any power of Satan be defeated. We don't have to work it up, make it up, or faith it up; the power is in the abiding presence of Jesus, who lives within us.

Part Two
The Supernatural

INTRODUCTION

In Part 1 of this book, I gave a brief history of the New Age Movement, showing how each of its founders was rejected by the Church and pushed into isolation in their pursuit to understand the supernatural. The result was deception and engagement with counterfeits of the supernatural power that God gives to all who accept Jesus as their Lord and Savior.

I also analyzed the biblical examples of power encounters, highlighting the shift in focus between the Old Testament and the New Testament. In the Old Testament, God established boundaries to help protect His people from outside corrupting forces. Those who purposefully rebelled against Him by operating in occult powers met with severe punishment. In the New Testament, the power encounters between Christians and those operating in false power had a different focus—rescuing people out of darkness and introducing them to the authentic power of Jesus.

As members of the New Covenant, our interactions with the practitioners of counterfeit supernatural power have the same thrust. We are not seeking to punish or humiliate or destroy; we are seeking to enlighten, embrace, and protect. With this purpose in mind, in Part 2 of this book, I will examine sixty-eight New Age supernatural practices and show them to be counterfeits of biblically-based, God-ordained supernatural power.

I've divided these into three basic sections: Elements of the Spirit Realm, Spiritual Insight, and Other Phenomenon. In these we will notice reoccurring themes and similarities even though each one adds a unique twist. Anyone familiar with the Bible will recognize that many supernatural events in the Bible do not fit into these categories; therefore, I have not covered them. Truly, our God is greater. As you read, remember that in John 14:12 Jesus told His followers, *"Truly, truly, I say to you, he who believes in Me, the works that I do, he will do also; and* **greater works than these** *he will do; because I go to the Father."* In other words, when it comes to the supernatural, we are not limited to what we read here or in the Bible. (We are, however, limited by the ethics and character of God as displayed in the Bible.) This is just the beginning of an incredible journey with the Holy Spirit. Supernatural gifts and abilities should never become our primary focus. Jesus is our focus, but He has given us these gifts for a purpose, and He wants us to earnestly pursue them! (See 1 Corinthians 12:31; 14:1.)

CHAPTER 5

ELEMENTS OF THE SPIRIT REALM

In this chapter I will highlight various beliefs about or aspects of the spirit world that are prominent in New Age teaching and practice, showing how each of these is a counterfeit understanding of God's true spirit realm as revealed in the Bible.

1. AFFIRMATIONS

Affirmation (n.) — A positive phrase or sentence that, through frequent repetition, uses the power of your mind to create a truth of reality. Affirmations are powerful verbal messages repeated over and over again so that they become embedded in your brain and create new pathways of thought and action.

We all know the incredible power inherent in our words. Life and death are in the power of the tongue (see Prov. 18:21). Negative and critical words can paralyze our potential to succeed in our calling, while encouraging and life-giving words can give us the boost we need to overcome the hurdles we face. It's as simple as that. The same is true of the words we speak to ourselves. Numerous studies have shown how greatly our words and the words we hear influence how we think and what we believe about ourselves and our world. However, this truth about the power of our words is not simply based on psychology and biology. It all started with God.

Hebrews 11:3 tells us God formed the universe *with His words*. He created new realities by speaking; when He said, *"Let there be light"* (Gen. 1:2), His words actually created light. Because we are made in the image of God, we also have creative power in our words. We don't create objects with our words, but we do create realities in people's hearts and minds.

Long before the recent popularity of the power of affirmations, the Bible revealed this same truth to God's people—only we call them *faith confessions*. The idea of declaring aloud a reality that we believe is God's will for us, but that we do not yet see manifest in the natural is based on verses like Joel 3:10, which says, *"...let the weak say, 'I am strong.'"* This is a faith confession that declares a new reality. In this verse, God is not telling the weak to find a way to become strong. He is telling them to declare their strength even though in the natural they are weak. He says to speak this reality forth because it is His destiny for them.

Similarly, in Isaiah 55, God tells us to speak our words out ahead of us so that when we arrive in our future, our words will have positively affected our future world.

Jesus also indicated the power of our words to change our reality when He said:

> *I tell you the truth, if anyone says to this mountain, "Go, throw yourself into the sea," and does not doubt in his heart but believes that what he says will happen, it will be done for him* (Mark 11:23).

The main difference between New Age affirmations and Christian faith confessions is the source of the power. Christians believe God will answer their words spoken in faith. They also believe God has given them creative power to release (prophesy) His truth—as it is already established in Heaven—into their earthly lives. This is what Jesus meant when He said, *"Truly I say to you, whatever you bind on earth shall have been bound in heaven; and whatever you loose on earth shall have been loosed in heaven"* (Matt. 18:18 NASB). It is our responsibility to imitate the reality of Heaven by declaring it on the earth. With our words, we have the power to bind evil (because Jesus already did it in Heaven), and we have the power to release all of the manifestations of God's goodness (because Jesus already did that, too).

This is so much more than the power of positive thinking. It is a declaration of the promises God has given us in the Bible. It is praying along with the Lord's Prayer—*"Your kingdom come. Your will be done, on earth as it is in heaven"* (Matt. 5:10 NASB)—and bringing Heaven to earth with our words.

2. Age of Aquarius

> **Age of Aquarius** (n.) — An astrological term denoting either the current or upcoming astrological age, depending on how one calculates. In popular culture, the Age of Aquarius refers to the advent of the New Age movement in the 1960s.

Astronomer and author David Williams claims that "the Age of Aquarius arrived about 1844,"[1] although there are varying opinions on its start date that range from the 1830s to the 1960s. Other astronomers believe the Age of Aquarius has not yet begun but that it will soon. Essentially, the Age of Aquarius is believed to be a time period in which the physical realm and the spirit realm have become so close that spirits and spiritual forces in the spirit realm are able to communicate with and influence the physical realm more than during any other time in history. The use of the term the *Age of Aquarius* has been all but replaced by the more modern term, the *New Age*.

This concept of an era in which spiritual activity is more prominent has been around a lot longer than many people realize, originating with the biblical term, *the last days*.

> *In the last days the mountain of the LORD's temple will be established as the highest of the mountains; it will be exalted above the hills, and all nations will stream to it* (Isaiah 2:2; Micah 4:1).

> *In the last days, God says, I will pour out my Spirit on all people. Your sons and daughters will prophesy, your young men will see visions, your old men will dream dreams* (Acts 2:17).

In these Scriptures, we see a promise of an era in history when the spirit realm will be more visibly involved on the earth and many people will turn to God and receive His Spirit, including a great outpouring of God's supernatural power. As the above verse from Acts 2 indicates, the last days arrived with the outpouring of the Spirit on Jesus' followers after His death and resurrection. In Acts 2, a small group of believers was baptized with the Holy Spirit as flames of fire rested above each of their heads and they began to speak in unknown tongues. In his sermon following this event, the apostle Peter quoted from Joel 2:28 to indicate that the outpouring of the Spirit they had just experienced was a sign that the last days had come.

The Church entered into a New Age with the Acts 2 day of Pentecost. We have been walking in the New Covenant Age ever since.

3. Akashic Records, the Book of the Dead

Akashic Records, the Book of the Dead (n.) — According to New Age teachings, the Akashic Records consist of extrasensory information that exists in another dimension, like the ultimate cosmic library. Some psychics say they consult the Akashic Records through clairvoyance or during out-of-body experiences (OBE).

Reading during an out-of-body experience is not an exclusively New Age concept. In fact, the Bible records multiple times when prophets were shown scrolls or books while in visions, trances, or OBEs (see Ezek. 2:8–3:15; Zech. 5; Rev. 10). Scripture also contains two significant accounts of spiritual books in the unseen realm that contain information about the lives of people on earth.

The first of these spirit books is the Book of Life, which the apostle John saw during his Revelation encounter:

> *Then I saw a great white throne and him who was seated on it. Earth and sky fled from his presence, and there was no place for them. And I saw the dead, great and small, standing before the throne, and* **books were opened. Another book was opened, which is the book of life.** *The dead were judged according to what they had done* **as recorded in the books.** *The sea gave up the dead that were in it, and death and Hades gave up the dead that were in them, and each person was judged according to what he had done. Then death and Hades were thrown into the lake of fire. The lake of fire is the second death. If anyone's name was not found written in the book of life, he was thrown into the lake of fire* (Revelation 20:11–15).

The second spirit book mentioned in the Bible is the Book of Remembrance, which was seen by the prophet Malachi:

> *Then those who feared the LORD spoke to one another, and the LORD listened and heard them; so **a book of remembrance was written before Him** for those who fear the LORD and who meditate on His name (Malachi 3:16).*

From these passages, we can see that the idea of spiritual books that contain the desires and destinies of humanity—as well as the idea that people sometimes view these books through spiritual experiences—is a very biblical one.

4. Astral Body

> **Astral Body** (n.) — According to shamans and Theosophists, in the astral realm (which is not normally visible to ordinary sight, yet is regarded as the proper dwelling of people's higher spiritual bodies), the astral body or second self resembles the physical body but is made up of a subtle field of shining and flexible light that encases the body, visible only by a psychically sensitive person. It is also known as the *Etheric Body*.

At first glance, this idea may seem very far from the reality of the Bible. However, if we can move past some of the "weirdness" of this New Age idea, we will see that it does in fact mirror a scriptural truth.

In the Bible, we learn that humankind was created in the image of God. One way in which we look like Him is in our trinity. God is three beings in one—Father, Son, and Holy Spirit. Like Him, we are also tri-part—body, soul, and spirit. We see this clearly spelled out at several places in the Bible, including First Thessalonians 5:23: *"May your whole spirit, soul and body be kept blameless at the coming of our Lord Jesus Christ."*

We are the way we are because we are like Him. God, too, is spirit (Holy Spirit), soul (the expressive and emotional nature of God the

Father), and body (Jesus as God in the flesh). What the New Age calls the Astral body is what the Bible calls the spirit of a person. This part of a person is invisible and interacts with the unseen realm. The spirit of a person has dreams, visions, and imaginations; it also interacts with spiritual beings and realms.

5. Astral Plane

> ***Astral Plane*** (n.) — According to occultists, the astral plane is an alternate and non-physical dimension of reality that can be visited during astral projection or out-of-body experiences. It is also known as the *Ether*.

Our physical bodies have a realm that they dwell in and interact with—the physical realm that we can see with our eyes. Likewise, our souls have a realm to dwell in and interact with—the interpersonal communication realm that we experience with our emotions and intellect. It follows that our spirits, too, have a realm to dwell in and interact with—the spiritual realm.

As I already stated, what the New Age refers to as the astral body, the Bible calls the spirit of a person. New Agers have named the dwelling of the so-called astral body the astral plane. The Bible calls it the spirit realm simply because it is the realm the human spirit interacts with. *"You, however, are not in the realm of the flesh but are in the realm of the Spirit, if indeed the Spirit of God lives in you"* (Rom. 8:9).

The apostle Paul talked about this when he enjoined the Corinthians to fix their attention on the spiritual realm and to live based on the realities they beheld there: *"So we fix our eyes not on what is seen, but on what is unseen. For what is seen is temporary, but what is unseen is eternal"* (2 Cor. 4:18).

From this verse, we learn two main features of the spirit realm. First, the spirit realm is invisible to the physical eye. Yet that does not mean it is unperceivable. Wind, gravity, and radio waves are all invisible to the naked eye, yet with the right equipment, we can prove their existence, study their behavior, and utilize their power. Similarly, our human spirits are the equipment we need to interact with the unseen realm. Through our spirits, we can learn and discern spiritual realities, and we can participate in the advancement of God's Kingdom on earth.

All three parts of our nature and the realms they occupy have a part to play in God's Kingdom, but for too long much of the Church has feared or ignored the spiritual realm. We follow a God who defined Himself as *Spirit* and instructed us to worship Him in spirit and in truth (see John 4:24). To do that, we must know how to interact with the spirit realm.

Second, we learn from Second Corinthians 4:18 that the spirit realm is an eternal realm. The physical world is temporary, but the spiritual realm will exist forever. We can say, then, that the spirit realm is the truer of the realms. In it we behold realities that will never fade away. Through it, we accomplish works that will bear fruit forever.

It is easy for us to understand reality based on the physical world our eyes see and the soul world of our minds and emotions. However, the Bible clearly calls us to live from another reality—the spiritual realm. It tells us that God *"raised us up with Him, and seated us with Him in the heavenly places in Christ Jesus"* (Eph. 2:6). In other words, as spiritual beings, Christians are called to live from the spirit realm and spiritual reality, to live, as Bill Johnson has famously put it, "from Heaven toward earth."[2] It is from our place in the spiritual realm that we understand our position as co-heirs with Christ who are seated at the right hand of the Father.

6. ASTROLOGY

> *Astrology* (n.) — An ancient system of divination that uses the positions of the moon, stars, and planets to interpret how movements in relation to each other affect our lives.

According to astrologers, celestial bodies exert forces and exhibit personalities that influence people and events on earth. These influences may be determined by mapping their positions in the sky at various points in times.

The Bible tells us that the stars and planets do indeed play an important role in human history, though not as astrologers claim. As a part of creation, the celestial bodies do not influence or direct people and events on earth. The Creator alone has that power. And this is exactly what the celestial bodies tell us. From the beginning of the universe, the stars and planets have communicated with humanity about the glory of God.

> *The heavens declare the glory of God; the skies proclaim the work of his hands. Day after day they pour forth speech; night after night they display knowledge. There is no speech or language where their voice is not heard. Their voice goes out into all the earth, their words to the ends of the world* (Psalm 19:1–14).

According to the psalmist, one of the chief jobs of the heavenly bodies is to proclaim the Creator. They are a universal declaration of His excellence and creative skill, and they also release knowledge of the Creator to the earth.

In fact, God even used the stars—through ancient astrology—to foretell the birth of His son and to lead several astrologers on a journey from the Middle East to locate the new born king of the Jews in Bethlehem (see Matt. 2:1–12). *"We saw his star when it rose and have come to worship him,"* the Magi said (Matt. 2:1). From this we can see that God can even use the stars and astronomy to tell us what He will do on the earth. Thus, it is not the stars themselves who influence the events of our lives (as astrologers would say). They are merely heralds of their Creator and ours.

7. AURA

> ***Aura*** (n.) — The enveloping energy that surrounds and radiates from natural objects, including human beings, animals, and plants. The colors and forms of each aura are believed to be characteristic of the person, animal, or thing it surrounds and to fluctuate and shift according to mood and state of health.

The New Age concept of *aura* is very similar to the *astral body,* with one exception. The term aura also implies the idea that individuals can carry a certain power within them. This, in fact, is a very biblical concept. The Bible teaches that the human spirit of a believer is literally one with the Holy Spirit: *"He who is joined to the Lord is one spirit with him"* (1 Cor. 6:17).

In other words, the human spirit radiates the power of the Holy Spirit through us wherever we go. In Scripture, healing seems to be the most common manifestation of how this power affects others. For example, the apostle Peter was known for radiating so much of the Spirit of God in his human spirit that people lined the streets in hopes that his shadow would touch and perhaps heal them.

> *As a result, people brought the sick into the streets and laid them on beds and mats so that at least Peter's shadow might fall on some of them as he passed by. Crowds gathered also from the towns around Jerusalem, bringing their sick and those tormented by evil spirits, and all of them were healed* (Acts 5:15–16).

From this biblical account, we can clearly see that spiritual substance can be carried in the spirit of a person and released to others. My friend, Chad Dedmon, has a modern story not unlike what happened to the apostle Peter. In the aftermath of Hurricane Katrina, Chad and some friends travelled to Houston to minister supernatural healing and encounters with Jesus to people. At one point, as Chad was talking with a woman, a man walked by within a few feet of them. As he passed, he turned and started yelling obscenities at Chad, saying, "What did you do to me?!!" Startled, Chad asked the man what he meant. As it turns out, when the man walked by Chad, he felt something like fire in his leg, and immediately all the pain he had suffered with, due to an injury in that leg, vanished. This man received supernatural healing simply by passing through the "aura" of the Holy Spirit that is resident within Chad and radiates out from him.[3]

Jesus also taught about the spiritual power we carry within us and can release around us. When He anointed and sent out seventy-two of His followers to preach the good news, He gave them instruction about the impact of the Spirit on the environment around them. This happened prior to His believers being filled with the Holy Spirit on the day of Pentecost, so when Jesus anointed them (put His Spirit upon them), He needed to tell them what would happen. He said, *"When you enter a house, first say, 'Peace to this house.' If someone who promotes peace is there, your peace will rest on them; if not, it will return to you"* (Luke 10:5–6). In this simple statement we find a compelling explanation of the power that dwells in us and that can flow out of us to impact the spiritual atmosphere around us.

This same Spirit lives inside every believer in Jesus, filling us with much more power than many of us realize. This is why the apostle Paul referred to us as *"a dwelling in which God lives by his Spirit"* (Eph. 2:22). Within us dwells the very potency of God.

8. Disciplines

> ***Disciplines*** *(n.)* — Tools used to promote self-control, quietness, awareness, and exploration. Generally, meditation, trances, prayer, consulting spirit guides and angels are all examples.

Spiritual disciplines are common to most religions, including Christianity. The Bible mentions many spiritual disciplines, including fasting, prayer, meditation, giving, Bible study, and worship. The two main differences between New Age disciplines and those practiced by Christians are:

1. **Focus**—New Agers focus their disciplines toward a variety of spirit entities or the Universe; Christians practice their disciplines unto the true God

2. **Purpose**—New Age disciplines are practiced with the purpose of gaining something (protection, power, healing, etc.) from a spirit entity; Christian disciplines are rooted in relationship and are performed in love and commitment to God, not as an effort to get something from Him

Paul wrote about the Christian purpose for discipline in one of his letters to Timothy:

> *On the other hand, discipline yourself for the purpose of godliness; for bodily discipline is only of little profit, but godliness is profitable for all things, since it holds promise for the present life and also for the life to come* (1 Timothy 4:7–8).

In other words, for the Christian, spiritual disciplines help cultivate spiritual growth. They help strengthen our intimacy with Jesus by bringing us into greater alignment with our new identity in

Him. When we accept Jesus as Lord, He gives us a new nature; we are no longer trapped by or inclined toward sin. With this new nature and with the Holy Spirit living within us, we are equipped to grow into the image of Christ. This happens through renewing our minds with the truth and through disciplining our hearts and habits toward our Father.

Christians use disciplines to align themselves with their new nature in Christ and to grow in intimacy with their Father. Disciplines are not (and should never be) about earning approval or gaining rewards. This is one of the core differences between Christianity and all other religions.

9. ELEMENTS

> ***Element*** (n.) — A natural or spiritual substance thought to be one of the fundamental energies of the universe with inherent power. Many belief systems have rituals and techniques to harness these energies and powers for boosting health or creating magic. Western traditions include four elements: air, water, fire, and earth.

The Bible reveals God as the creator of the heavens and the earth and the ruler of the elements. As God says in Isaiah 48:13, *"My own hand laid the foundations of the earth, and my right hand spread out the heavens; when I summon them, they all stand up together."* In other words, God has the power to interrupt the normal course of the elements and seasons when He pleases. In various places in the Bible, we see Him give this power to His followers as well.

In the Book of Joshua, the Israelites were fighting against the Amorites, and they needed more daylight to win the battle. This is what happened:

> *On the day the LORD gave the Amorites over to Israel, Joshua said to the LORD in the presence of Israel: "O sun, stand still over Gibeon, O moon, over the Valley of Aijalon." So the sun stood still, and the moon stopped, till the nation avenged itself on its enemies, as it is written in the Book of Jashar. The sun stopped in the middle of the sky and delayed going down about a full day. There has never been a day like it before or since, a day when the LORD listened to a man. Surely the LORD was fighting for Israel* (Joshua 10:12–14).

While this sort of intervention is not common, as this passage indicates, it is possible. We find another slightly less dramatic example in the Book of Isaiah, when the prophet uses the backward progression of the sun as a supernatural sign to confirm his prophetic word: "'*I will make the shadow cast by the sun go back the ten steps it has gone down on the stairway of Ahaz.' So the sunlight went back the ten steps it had gone down*" (Isa. 38:8).

Similarly, the prophet Elijah stopped the rain over the land of Israel for three years to substantiate his prophecies calling the nation to stop serving false gods. At the end of three years, after a dramatic power encounter with the priests of the false gods, Elijah prayed and released the rain (see 1 Kings 17–18). In the New Testament, the apostle James applied the power to influence the elements to every follower of Jesus:

> *Elijah was a man just like us. He prayed earnestly that it would not rain, and it did not rain on the land for three and a half years. Again he prayed, and the heavens gave rain, and the earth produced its crops* (James 5:17–18).

Jesus also demonstrated our power over the elements when he calmed a storm:

> *Then he got into the boat and his disciples followed him. Without warning, a furious storm came up on the lake, so that the waves swept over the boat. But Jesus was sleeping. The disciples went and woke him, saying, "Lord, save us! We're going to drown!" He replied, "You of little faith, why are you so afraid?" Then he got up and rebuked the winds and the waves, and it was completely calm. The men were amazed and asked, "What kind of man is this? Even the winds and the waves obey him"* (Matthew 8:23–27).

In Jesus' rebuke to His disciples regarding their lack of faith, we see that He had expected *them* to calm the storm. The Holy Spirit within followers of Jesus gives us the ability to command even the elements to obey us.

10. Elementals

> ***Elementals*** **(n.)** — Indo-European nature spirits or angels that are believed to be manifestations of the four elements: water, air, fire, and earth. In modern magical philosophy, elementals are seen as conscious elements inhabiting the physical world. They have extensive powers over the elements they indwell, and their powers are at the disposal of the magician who has mastered the elemental force within (also called Devas).

This New Age concept of Elementals (which is closely connected to the previous section, Elements) parallels a much greater biblical truth regarding our identity as children of God. When God created humankind, the Bible records:

> *And the LORD God formed man of the dust of the ground, and breathed into his nostrils the breath of life; and man became a living being* (Genesis 2:7).

In other words, God used the elements of the earth to create the human race. He started with dirt (earth) and formed it into the divine image. Though the text doesn't say it, we can intuit here the presence of water to make the dry dust into a moldable mud. Then He breathed on it, releasing both air and spirit. Thus humanity was born from the elements of earth, water, and air and made distinct from all the other creatures by the addition of fire, which is the spirit inside each person.

In Hebrews 12:29, which quotes Deuteronomy 4:24, God refers to Himself as a *"consuming fire."* We are made in His image, and we have His divine fire within us. This is the spiritual nature of all humans, whether they know God or not. It is a part of how He made us.

The Bible also talks about the miracle of salvation in metaphors using the elements water, wind, and fire. In speaking of Jesus' ministry, John the Baptist said, *"He will baptize you with the Holy Spirit and fire"* (Luke 3:16). Referring to the new life He gives us, Jesus said, *"Whoever drinks the water I give him will never thirst"* and *"the water I give him will become in him a spring of water welling up to eternal life"* (John 4:13–14; see also John 7:37–39). He also said His followers must be *"born of water* [natural birth] *and the Spirit* [spiritual birth]*"* (John 3:5) and that this spiritual birth would make them very much like the wind:

> *The wind blows wherever it pleases. You hear its sound, but you cannot tell where it comes from or where it is going. So it is with everyone born of the Spirit* (John 3:8).

The point of all this is that new covenant believers are filled with the very elements of the Creator who created earth, air, wind, and fire. And this isn't just a nice-sounding idea either. With it comes real power over the elements of the natural world. Like Elijah, who commanded the rain (see 1 Kings 17:1); like Joshua, who commanded the sun (see Josh. 10:13); and like Jesus, who commanded the wind and waves (see Matt. 8:26), followers of God have authority over nature for the purpose of averting storms, preventing natural disasters, and the like.

This is something the Church still needs a lot of growth in, but the Bible tells us it is part of our inheritance as children of God. Jesus made that clear in Matthew 17:20, when He told His disciples:

> *Truly I tell you, if you have faith as small as a mustard seed, you can say to this mountain, "Move from here to there," and it will move. Nothing will be impossible for you.*

In fact, I believe this ability to command the elements is part of God's solution for the terrible acts of nature that often happen in this fallen world. Instead of blaming natural disasters on God, we should stand up as the children of God we are and command these disasters to dissipate in the name of Jesus.

11. Guided Visualization

> ***Guided Visualization or Imagery*** (n.) — A kind of directed daydreaming, creative visualization, hypnosis, or meditation that allows people to enter a state in which they can picture and experience images that help to heal or motivate them.

Visualization can look like a cancer patient picturing army tanks shooting down cancer cells or a sprinter imagining the speed and grace of a cheetah. In other words, the imagination is used in a directed way to help a person achieve goals. Though some Christians would view this as dangerous territory, the Bible actually talks about visualizing heavenly spiritual realities in order to see them manifest in our physical experience. We see this first in the story of Abraham, who was instructed by God to count the stars as an act of imagining the number of his descendants (see Gen. 15:5).

In Joshua 1:8, God told Joshua to meditate on His Word day and night so that he would be able to follow it and, as a result, become prosperous and successful. The concept of meditation inherently includes within it the idea of visualization, since our minds naturally create images to accompany whatever it is we are thinking about. It is not surprising, then, that the Hebrew word translated as "meditate" in this passage can also be translated as "imagine."[4]

The Bible not only instructs us to meditate on God's truth but also confirms the fact that what we think about and imagine tends to manifest in tangible ways in our lives. *"For as he thinks within himself, so he is"* (Prov. 23:7a NASB). This is true even when people are unconscious of it. Many books have catalogued this phenomenon, and self-help and New Age gurus have encouraged their followers to use what they call "the law of attraction" to fulfill their desires. Obviously, this is the counterfeit of the power of godly imagination, as we can see in the difference in focus. One is motivated by a focus on self; the other is motivated, in partnership with the Holy Spirit, by the desire to fulfill destiny.

When we intentionally use our imaginations to accomplish God's will for our lives, the power of godly visualization is magnified. In Second Corinthians 3:18, Paul described it this way:

> *And we all, who with unveiled faces contemplate the Lord's glory, are being transformed into his image with ever-increasing glory, which comes from the Lord, who is the Spirit.*

This is how we become like Christ, by using our imaginations to visualize His glory. Paul was not talking here about literally, with our physical eyes, contemplating the Lord's glory. He was talking about using our imaginations. The apostle Paul also wrote:

> *Since then, you have been raised with Christ, set your hearts on things above, where Christ is seated at the right*

hand of God. Set your minds on things above, not on earthly things (Colossians 3:1–2).

In other words, we use our imaginations to connect our minds with the divine realities in Heaven.

12. Home Circle

Home Circle (n.) — A meeting of a group of people who wish to communicate with spirits of loved ones or other supernatural entities. It is also known as a *home sitting*. This is a séance that is held in a private home, it is led by a medium who acts as a go-between for the group and the spirits. The main purpose of a home circle is to communicate with spirits.

Once again, we find that God first ordained groups meeting in homes to connect with the spirit world (to connect with God the Father through the Holy Spirit). After the formation of the early Church, people regularly met together in their houses for spiritual fellowship, including prayer and worship (see Acts 2:46; 5:42). From the beginning, communication with God has not been confined to church buildings or sacred locations because we, as members of the Church, are the dwelling place of the Holy Spirit (see 1 Cor. 3:16). It follows, then, that wherever we are is a good place to communicate with Him.

One very remarkable instance of this is recorded in Acts 10. The apostle Peter was summoned to the house of a Roman centurion, Cornelius, who was not a believer in Jesus. An angel had appeared to Cornelius, telling him to send for Peter. When Peter arrived at Cornelius' house, he discovered a large group of people awaiting his teaching. As Peter began to tell them about Jesus, the Holy Spirit filled the room, and Cornelius and his friends and family were filled with the Holy Spirit. Here we see unbelievers having their first encounter with the Holy Spirit in a small home gathering. This pattern has continued throughout history and is still common today.

13. Imagination

> ***Imagination*** (n.) — The ability to visualize and make sense of the universe in pictures and symbols, not words.

Similar to guided visualization, imagination is something that comes from within a person's own mind and involves images and sensations that do not demonstrate any basis in reality. As we discussed before, the Bible gives much evidence for the importance of using our imaginations. Here I will highlight a few supplemental passages. First, look at this statement from Jesus:

> *You have heard that it was said, "Do not commit adultery." But I tell you that anyone who looks at a woman lustfully has already committed adultery with her in his heart* (Matthew 5:27-28).

Here, Jesus said that imagining an act is the same as doing it in real life. When He said adultery is committed in the heart, He was referring to the human imagination. This is an example of using the imagination in meditation in the negative sense. Yet it validates the power and legitimacy of the imagination, showing that it has a reality to it. As the poet William Blake wrote, "What is now proved was once only imagined."[5] Imagination is the creative organ of our spirits. For example, all inventions in the earth have come from someone's imagination. Even when God determined to create the earth and each person on the earth, He must have first imagined what He was creating. That is simply how our minds work. God has quite an imagination!

Second, look at Paul's words to the Ephesians:

I pray that the eyes of your heart may be enlightened *in order that you may know the hope to which He has called you, the riches of His glorious inheritance in the saints* (Ephesians 1:18).

What does it mean for the eyes of our hearts to be enlightened? I believe Paul was talking about using our imaginations in partnership with the Holy Spirit. Clearly, Paul put great value on receiving enlightenment for our spiritual eyes. Unfortunately, although the first century Church understood the importance of the imagination, much of the modern Church has made it a low priority.

14. Initiation Rites

Initiation Rites (n.) — Individual transformation that involves a transition from one level of awareness to the next.

Initiation rituals designed to stimulate transformation have existed since ancient times, ranging from coming-of-age initiations at puberty to the elaborate ceremonies of Freemasonry, by which members advance to the next grade or degree and receive the teaching, rights, and formal title of that level of membership.

The obvious biblical parallel to such initiation rites is the outward act of baptism, which symbolizes the believer's death with Christ and resurrection into new life. John the Baptist baptized people in preparation for Jesus' ministry. When Jesus began His ministry, He had His disciples baptize His followers. After His resurrection, before He ascended back into Heaven, Jesus promised a new sort of baptism to His followers—the baptism of the Holy Spirit (see Acts 1:5). After this happened on the day of Pentecost (see Acts 2), the early Church connected the outward physical baptism in water with the spiritual baptism in the Holy Spirit:

> *Repent, and each of you be baptized in the name of Jesus Christ for the forgiveness of your sins; and you will receive the gift of the Holy Spirit* (Acts 2:38).

This pattern of baptizing new believers continued throughout the New Testament, and it is still common practice in the Church today. This is the primary initiation rite of biblical Christianity.

However, as we see in the example of the Freemasons, sometimes initiation rites are also used to bring members into increasing levels within the group. This is a progressive initiation into a fuller understanding and transformation. Christianity, too, contains this progression from the "elementary teachings" to "maturity." It is not accompanied by any outward ritual, but it is a definite progression all believers are to make in the renewing of their minds (see Rom. 12:2; Eph. 4:23). The elementary teachings are listed here:

> *Therefore let us leave the elementary teachings about Christ and go on to maturity, not laying again the foundation of repentance from acts that lead to death, and of faith in God, instruction about baptisms, the laying on of hands, the resurrection of the dead, and eternal judgment* (Hebrews 6:1–2).

From this passage it is clear that believers are expected to progressively grow in understanding and in transformation into the character of Christ.

15. Invocation or Evocation

Invocation (n.) — The act of calling a deity or other spiritual power into a medium, magician, or witch. The word is taken from the Latin *advoco*, meaning "summon."

Evocation (n.) — The process of summoning a spirit into some form of manifestation that is external to the medium.

The concepts of invocation and evocation are present throughout Scripture, related to evil spirits as well as to the Spirit of God. When people invite a spirit other than the Holy Spirit into themselves or to manifest in their presence, they are entering into dangerous territory. Many mediums, witches, and the like invite spirits into their lives in order to gain spiritual power, but in the process, they become slaves to a hostile force that will eventually destroy them (see Rom. 6:16).

The Bible also talks a great deal about inviting the Holy Spirit into our lives. In the Old Testament, people often called upon the Lord for help in difficult times or for wisdom to make the right decision. We see this illustrated in the Psalms:

> *Bow Your heavens, O LORD, and come down; touch the mountains, that they may smoke* (Psalm 144:5).
>
> *I call upon the LORD, who is worthy to be praised, and I am saved from my enemies. …In my distress I called upon the LORD, yes, I cried to my God; and from His temple He heard my voice, and my cry for help came into His ears* (2 Samuel 22:4,7).
>
> *The LORD is near to all who call upon Him, to all who call upon Him in truth* (Psalm 145:18).

The prophet Ezekiel was one of the rare Old Testament figures who experienced the Spirit of God entering him—and in quite a dramatic fashion:

> *Then He said to me, "Son of man, stand on your feet that I may speak with you!" As He spoke to me the Spirit entered me and set me on my feet; and I heard Him speaking to me* (Ezekiel 2:1–2).

In the New Testament, because of the death and resurrection of Jesus, all people are now able to invite the Holy Spirit to dwell within them. Thus, the apostle Paul wrote to the Corinthian Christians: *"Do you not know that you are a temple of God and that the Spirit of God dwells in you?"* (1 Cor. 3:16).

Similarly, in Galatians 4:6, he wrote, *"Because you are sons, God has sent forth the Spirit of His Son into our hearts, crying, "Abba! Father!"* When we invite the Holy Spirit to dwell inside us, He does give us supernatural power, but He also gives us life and freedom.

That's amazing! Yet Jesus took this concept one step farther, saying not only would His followers be filled with the Spirit, but God would actually speak through them:

> *But when they hand you over, do not worry about how or what you are to say; for it will be given you in that hour what you are to say. For it is not you who speak, but it is the Spirit of your Father who speaks in you* (Matthew 10:19–20).

Many believers throughout history who have been filled with the Spirit of God have also experienced God filling their mouths with His words. What an incredible privilege it is for us humans to speak the very words of God.

16. KARMA

> ***Karma*** (n.) — The universal principle, according to Hinduism, of cause and effect, action and reaction, that governs all life. In Hinduism, *karma* literally means "deed" or "act." It is not fate, for people act with free will and create their own destiny.

The concept behind karma—which Christians often refer to as "sowing and reaping"—is found throughout Scripture. In Proverbs, it says:

> *He who sows iniquity will reap vanity, and the rod of his fury will perish. He who is generous will be blessed, for he gives some of his food to the poor (Proverbs 22:8–9).*

In the New Testament, the apostle Paul twice addressed this universal system of cause and effect and the way it applies to our lives as Christians:

> *Do not be deceived: God cannot be mocked. A man reaps what he sows. The one who sows to please his sinful nature, from that nature will reap destruction; the one who sows to please the Spirit, from the Spirit will reap eternal life. Let us not become weary in doing good, for at the proper time we will reap a harvest if we do not give up (Galatians 6:7–9).*

> *Now this I say, he who sows sparingly will also reap sparingly, and he who sows bountifully will also reap bountifully (2 Corinthians 9:6).*

However, the Bible also makes it clear that we can rise above the negative side of the sowing and reaping principle through repentance for sins. Hinduism offers no grace to cover over past actions. But through Christ, we can find forgiveness for our sins—a forgiveness that removes the curse of past actions and enables us to begin sowing rightly.

17. MEDITATION

> ***Meditation*** (n.) — A contemplative technique in which people focus their concentration on a specific object or thought for self-improvement or spiritual growth.

The Bible says quite a bit about meditation, particularly on the following things:

The Lord Himself

On my bed I remember you; I think of you through the watches of the night (Psalm 63:6).

The Word of God

Keep this Book of the Law always on your lips; meditate on it day and night, so that you may be careful to do everything written in it. Then you will be prosperous and successful (Joshua 1:8).

The Works of God

I will remember the deeds of the LORD; yes, I will remember your miracles of long ago. I will consider all your works and meditate on all your mighty deeds (Psalm 77:11–12).

I remember the days of long ago; I meditate on all your works and consider what your hands have done (Psalm 143:5).

Good things

Finally, brothers and sisters, whatever is true, whatever is noble, whatever is right, whatever is pure, whatever is lovely, whatever is admirable—if anything is excellent or praiseworthy—think about such things (Philippians 4:8).

Prophetic Words

Do not neglect your gift, which was given you through prophecy when the body of elders laid their hands on you.

Be diligent in these matters; give yourself wholly to them, so that everyone may see your progress (1 Timothy 4:14–15).

18. Necromancy

Necromancy (n.) — The conjuring or summoning of spirits of the dead for magical purposes. Often considered dangerous and unwholesome, necromancy is a universal and ancient practice based on the belief that the dead, unrestricted by human limitations, are able to see into the past, present, and future and, if conjured and questioned, can tell what lies ahead.

The Bible does not endorse necromancy, but it does contain several instances in which dead people appeared to humans living on earth. It also seems to confirm the belief that the dead (at least those in Heaven) are able to observe some of the events on earth:

Therefore we also, **since we are surrounded by so great a cloud of witnesses**, *let us lay aside every weight, and the sin which so easily ensnares us, and let us run with endurance the race that is set before us* (Hebrews 12:1).

The Old Testament law prohibited trying to contact the dead, and any who engaged in such practices were to be expelled from Israel (see Deut. 18:10–12). King Saul deliberately went against that law when he consulted a medium, asking her to call up the spirit of the dead prophet Samuel (see 1 Sam. 28:7–19). The medium called up Samuel, but when she saw him, she responded in shock and fear. Clearly, this was outside the scope of what she had experienced before. In other words, we can assume from this passage that in the past, when this medium had called up spirits from the dead, she had not actually been consulting with dead humans. Thus, when the literal spirit of Samuel appeared, she was terrified, describing him as *"a divine being coming up out of the earth"* (1 Sam. 28:13).

This is pretty clear evidence that necromancy does not actually call up dead people but, instead, evil spirits that impersonate them. Saul's encounter was different. When Samuel rebuked Saul and prophesied his death on the very next day, he delivered a word from God to Saul that was fulfilled within twenty-four hours. Therefore, it seems clear it was actually Samuel in this instance, not an impersonating spirit. In fact, I believe in this instance God hijacked the medium's ritual by *actually* allowing Samuel to appear instead of the usual deceiving spirit.

A second instance in Scripture of dead people appearing on earth happened when Jesus was transfigured and the prophets from long ago, Moses and Elijah, appeared with Him.

> *After six days Jesus took with him Peter, James and John the brother of James, and led them up a high mountain by themselves. There he was transfigured before them. His face shone like the sun, and his clothes became as white as the light. Just then there appeared before them Moses and Elijah, talking with Jesus.*
>
> *Peter said to Jesus, "Lord, it is good for us to be here. If you wish, I will put up three shelters—one for you, one for Moses and one for Elijah."*
>
> *While he was still speaking, a bright cloud enveloped them, and a voice from the cloud said, "This is my Son, whom I love; with him I am well pleased. Listen to him!"*
>
> *When the disciples heard this, they fell facedown to the ground, terrified. But Jesus came and touched them. "Get up," he said. "Don't be afraid." When they looked up, they saw no one except Jesus* (Matthew 17:1–8).

Here, it's important to note that Moses and Elijah were not summoned, but they appeared as part of God's divine plan for Jesus' life.

A third instance happened during the apostle John's epic visionary encounter, in which he went to Heaven and received knowledge of future events. These he then recorded in the Book of Revelation. During this experience, John received information from angels and from a human living in Heaven (i.e. a dead person):

> *Then he said to me, "Write: 'Blessed are those who are called to the marriage supper of the Lamb!'" And he said to me, "These are the true sayings of God." And I fell at his feet to worship him. But he said to me, "See that you do not do that!* ***I am your fellow servant, and of your brethren who have the testimony of Jesus.*** *Worship God! For the testimony of Jesus is the spirit of prophecy"* (Revelation 19:9–10).

From these three instances, we see that spirits of dead humans can appear on earth and also that we can see and interact with them during experiences in Heaven (see the section on out-of-body experiences for more on this). But here's the catch—it may happen only by God's bidding. When people use necromancy to attempt to contact the dead, they are trespassing on dangerous spiritual territory.

19. NEW AGE

> ***New Age*** (n.) — An umbrella term used to describe a movement that encompasses a broad range of Eastern and Western interests in mysticism, spiritualism, religion, health, parapsychology, ecology, philosophy, self-development, and the occult.

The term *New Age* replaced the Age of Aquarius label used in the 1960s to describe the astrologically predicted dawning of a new age characterized by spiritualism, intuition, and revolutionary new ways of thinking. As I discussed in Chapter 1, the term *New Age* can encompass many different sorts of beliefs, including witchcraft, animism, shamanism, and others. These are not unlike the Old Testament division of God's people into twelve tribes and the modern clustering of Christians into various denominations or groups based upon common core beliefs.

Even in the first century Church, believers tended to gather into these distinct groups. Paul addressed this when he wrote:

> For when one says, "I follow Paul," and another, "I follow Apollos," are you not mere human beings? What, after all, is Apollos? And what is Paul? Only servants, through whom you came to believe—as the Lord has assigned to each his task. I planted the seed, Apollos watered it, but God has been making it grow. So neither the one who plants nor the one who waters is anything, but only God, who makes things grow. The one who plants and the one who waters have one purpose, and they will each be rewarded according to their own labor. For we are co-workers in God's service; you are God's field, God's building (1 Corinthians 3:4–9).

Paul's point here is that all these groups are still part of one body and one purpose. They are united together in Christ and have no cause for divisiveness.

20. Numerology

> ***Numerology*** (n.) — A system through which names, birthdates, and birthplaces are reduced to numbers in order to determine a person's personality and destiny.

Numerology is based on the belief that the universe is mathematically constructed and that the vibrational energy of people, places, and things can be expressed through numbers. It is like the concept behind Astrology, except with numbers instead of stars. Not surprisingly, the Bible (especially the Old Testament) uses numbers in a significant way, for example the seventy times seven of Daniel's prophecies and the infamous 666 of Revelation. In fact, because each Hebrew letter also has a numerical value, many Jews use a type of numerology called Gematria to interpret the Torah through mathematical formulations.

The Bible uses numbers symbolically, yet it is important to note that the numbers themselves do not contain any spiritual power or divinity. They do not have intelligence, as some New Age practitioners believe. Like the stars, they are simply tools in the hands of the God so magnificent that He created and fully comprehends the truth and beauty of mathematics, which some say is the purest form of intelligence.

21. Prayer

> ***Prayer*** *(n.) — A form of communication, distant healing, or thought projection with the divine or supernatural. The simplest forms of prayer are requests for yourself or others. These are directions of psychic energy toward a goal and involve words, symbols, and images.*

Prayer, as defined in the Bible, is simply human communication with God, and it has been part of human history since the creation of the universe. The Bible records many individual prayers and instances of people praying. The most famous of these is the Lord's Prayer, which Jesus used to teach His disciples how to pray:

> *Our Father who is in heaven, hallowed be Your name. Your kingdom come. Your will be done, on earth as it is in heaven. Give us this day our daily bread. And forgive us our debts, as we also have forgiven our debtors. And do*

not lead us into temptation, but deliver us from evil. For Yours is the kingdom and the power and the glory forever. Amen (Matthew 6:9–13 NASB).

What sets Christian prayer apart from all other forms of prayer? The expectation of an answer. Those who follow Jesus confidently believe that when they pray, He hears them and answers:

This is the confidence which we have before Him, that, if we ask anything according to His will, He hears us. And if we know that He hears us in whatever we ask, we know that we have the requests which we have asked from Him (1 John 5:14–15).

No other religion can claim this. The prophet Elijah illustrated this well in his show-down with the prophets of Baal on Mount Carmel (see Chapter 3). Elijah taunted the prophets of Baal for their inability to make their god hear and respond to their prayers and shouts and self-flagellation. They tried, for many hours, to elicit a response, but to no effect. Elijah, however, said a simple prayer, and God answered immediately and miraculously (see 1 Kings 18:20–40).

22. SILVER CORD

Silver Cord (n.) — A silver thread that acts as a connecting link between the physical and the astral body that has been reportedly seen by some practitioners of astral projection.

The Bible actually specifically mentions the silver cord in the context of death, indicating that when the cord is broken, the dust (human body) returns to the earth (decays) and the spirit returns to God:

Remember Him before the silver cord is broken and the golden bowl is crushed, the pitcher by the well is shattered and the wheel at the cistern is crushed; then the dust will return to the earth as it was, and the spirit will return to God who gave it (Ecclesiastes 12:6–7).

This cord, then, ties the physical to the spiritual, enabling the physical body to live. It is also mentioned in the Book of Job, in Eliphaz's discourse on the wicked. He describes their death in this way: *"Is not their tent-cord plucked up within them?"* (Job 4:21).

23. SMUDGING

Smudging (n.) — A Native North American practice of cleansing an environment with an ancient smoke ritual. It involves burning small bundles of herbs and sweet smelling grasses to physically and spiritually cleanse homes and people, replacing negative energy with positive. It is also called *Cleansing a Room*.

The Bible says a great deal about the need for cleansing, both for individuals and for locations. The most famous instance of this happened when the Israelite slaves in Egypt cleansed their homes by placing lamb's blood on the doorposts. This, God told them, would protect them from the judgment that was about to fall upon the Egyptians:

Then they are to take some of the blood and put it on the sides and tops of the doorframes of the houses.... On that same night I will pass through Egypt and strike down every firstborn—both men and animals—and I will bring judgment on all the gods of Egypt. I am the LORD. The blood will be a sign for you on the houses where you are; and when I see the blood, I will pass over you. No destructive plague will touch you when I strike Egypt (Exodus 12:7, 12–13),

The Old Testament law also gave directions for how to cleanse a house that had been contaminated with unclean objects:

> *To cleanse the house then, he shall take two birds and cedar wood and a scarlet string and hyssop, and he shall slaughter the one bird in an earthenware vessel over running water. Then he shall take the cedar wood and the hyssop and the scarlet string, with the live bird, and dip them in the blood of the slain bird as well as in the running water, and sprinkle the house seven times. He shall thus cleanse the house with the blood of the bird and with the running water, along with the live bird and with the cedar wood and with the hyssop and with the scarlet string* (Leviticus 14:49–52).

During one of the revivals of Israel, King Hezekiah ordered the temple cleansed, and the priests spent eight days cleansing the temple from all impurities (see 2 Chron. 29:12–19). Later, Nehemiah had the temple cleansed after a foreigner contaminated it (see Neh. 13:4–9). In the Old Testament, cleansing always involved the blood of an animal, which was symbolic of God's forgiveness of sins and spiritual cleansing power.

In the New Testament, this manifested in the death and resurrection of Jesus, who forever provided forgiveness of sins and cleansing from impurity for all who would receive it (see Heb. 9:14; 1 John 1:9). Thus, in the New Testament, believers in Jesus do not need the blood of animals or other items and rituals to cleanse an environment. We carry the cleansing power of Jesus within us, and we are able to release it wherever we go.

Jesus illustrated this for us when He cleansed the temple just prior to His death. The Jews had been using the temple for a profit, charging people exorbitant fees to purchase sacrifices and the like. By doing this, they were keeping the people from God. Jesus drove them out, and then He healed a bunch of blind and lame people while the children shouted worship to God. He didn't need to make a sacrifice or apply blood to anything. The Spirit resting on Jesus cleansed the temple and created an atmosphere in which people could encounter God (see Matt. 21:12–17). Unfortunately, the Jews quickly returned the temple to its former condition.

24. Spirit Guide

> **Spirit Guide** (n.) — A discarnate entity, often perceived as the higher self or a spirit of the dead that serves as a communications bridge, guardian, or guide. It is also known as a *totem spirit* or a *familiar spirit*. In shamanism the spirit guide is known as a *totem animal*, in spiritualism it is known as the *medium's control*, while in witchcraft it is known as a *familiar*.

In the Bible, the concept of a spirit guide is manifested in the Holy Spirit, who lives inside all believers. This is what Jesus had to say about the Holy Spirit:

> *I will ask the Father, and He will give you another Helper, that He may be with you forever; that is the Spirit of truth, whom the world cannot receive, because it does not see Him or know Him, but you know Him because He abides with you and will be in you* (John 14:16–17).
>
> *The Helper, the Holy Spirit, whom the Father will send in My name, He will teach you all things, and bring to your remembrance all that I said to you* (John 14:26).
>
> *When the Helper comes, whom I will send to you from the Father, that is the Spirit of truth who proceeds from the Father, He will testify about Me* (John 15:26).
>
> *I have many more things to say to you, but you cannot bear them now. But when He, the Spirit of truth, comes,*

> *He will guide you into all the truth; for He will not speak on His own initiative, but whatever He hears, He will speak; and He will disclose to you what is to come. He will glorify Me, for He will take of Mine and will disclose it to you* (John 16:12–14).

The Holy Spirit, the Spirit of God, lives within us as a divine helper, comforter, and teacher. He also empowers us with the very power of God (see Rom. 8:11). He is so much more than a spirit guide; He is a friend.

25. Trances

> **Trance** (n.) — A state between sleeping and waking, when a person is half conscious, is focusing exclusively on internal thoughts and visions, and is unaware of what is going on around that person.

In Greek, the word for *trance* means "a displacement of the mind."[6] This is the word used to describe what happened to the apostle Peter in Acts 10:

> *About noon the following day as they were on their journey and approaching the city, Peter went up on the roof to pray. He became hungry and wanted something to eat, and while the meal was being prepared, he fell into a trance. He saw heaven opened and something like a large sheet being let down to earth by its four corners. It contained all kinds of four-footed animals, as well as reptiles of the earth and birds of the air* (Acts 10:9–12; see also Acts 11:5).

The apostle Paul also had a trance in which Jesus appeared to him and gave him a message:

When I returned to Jerusalem and was praying at the temple, I fell into a trance and saw the Lord speaking. "Quick!" he said to me. "Leave Jerusalem immediately, because they will not accept your testimony about me" (Acts 22:17-18).

In these passages, we clearly see that trances are one way in which God can and does communicate with His followers.

26. Universal Life Force

Universal Life Force (n.) — The force upon which all things depend for health and life, which transcends time and space and permeates all things. It is also called *universal energy, vital force, vibrations, spiritual energy,* and *Chi, Qi, Ki.*

According to science, all atoms (except Hydrogen atoms) contain at least one proton, neutron, and electron. Protons and electrons are opposing charges. Protons and electrons attract each other, but protons repel other protons and electrons repel other electrons. Yet, protons are held together in the nucleus of each atom. Every nucleus should be splitting because of the way protons repel each other. The question of *what* holds together the protons in every atom is one of the great mysteries of science.

The New Age explains this mystery by referring to a force—the Universal Life Force—that holds all things together. Similarly, on the atomic level, they also recognize an energy that they refer to as *spiritual energy.* The Bible confirms both of these as facts. God is the one who holds the entire universe together, including every atom. Paul explained this mystery when he wrote, *"He is before all things, and in Him all things hold together"* (Col. 1:17 NASB). God is the glue of the universe. Only by His power are the many elements that make up this physical reality held together in a meaningful way.

This is profound. What is most incredible is that God has put this same universe-holding-together power inside His followers, and He works through us to enact His desires (and our desires) on the earth. Paul said he worked with God's very energy in order to expand His Kingdom. *"For this I toil, struggling with all his energy that he powerfully works within me"* (Col. 1:29 ESV). It is both humbling and comforting to know that the same force who holds the universe together also lives inside of us and calls us His friends.

Chapter 6

Spiritual Insight

In this chapter, I will focus on spiritual experiences related to receiving knowledge about the past, present, or future through spiritual means. The New Age focuses quite a bit on this ability to hear and see and learn in the spirit realm, and so does the Bible—but with some key differences.

27. Channeling

> ***Channeling*** (n.) — The process through which a medium communicates information from spirits and other non-physical beings, such as angels, deities, or guardian spirits, by entering into a trance or some other altered state of consciousness.

The New Age concept of channeling is, in fact, very similar to the experiences of some biblical prophets and the way in which they delivered messages from God to His people. For example, in First Kings 22, Micaiah prophecies to the evil King Ahab by relaying a message he received while in the throne room of God in Heaven:

> *Micaiah said, "Therefore, hear the word of the LORD. I saw the LORD sitting on His throne, and all the host of heaven standing by Him on His right and on His left. The LORD said, 'Who will entice Ahab to go up and fall at Ramoth-gilead?' And one said this while another said that. Then a spirit came forward and stood before the LORD and said, 'I will entice him.' The LORD said to him, 'How?' And he said, 'I will go out and be a deceiving spirit in the mouth of all his prophets.' Then He said, 'You are to entice him and also prevail. Go and do so.' Now therefore, behold, the LORD has put a deceiving spirit in the mouth of all these your prophets; and the LORD has proclaimed disaster against you"* (1 Kings 22:19–23 NASB; see also 2 Chronicles 18:18–22).

Similarly, in Zachariah 3:1–7, the prophet relays a message from God based on what he heard and saw in the throne room in Heaven. Job 1 also relays a story from the throne room. In the New Testament, the apostle John received an entire book of prophecy, the Book of Revelation, in this way. He saw events happen and heard them explained in the heavenly realms; then he wrote them down in a book for the people of his day.[1]

In the Old Covenant, this sort of experience was reserved for select prophets of the Lord. However, in the New Covenant, all who have accepted Jesus as their Lord are filled with the Spirit of God and commissioned as ambassadors of Heaven to communicate messages from God to the people of earth. The apostle Paul said it this way: *"Now then, we are ambassadors for Christ, as though God were pleading through us: we implore you on Christ's behalf, be reconciled to God"* (2 Corinthians 5:20).

In other words, as believers in Christ, we have become the conduit—the channel, if you will—for God's communications from the spirit realm into the earthly realm. This is not an impersonal experience in which the Spirit takes control of our bodies (as in the New Age counterfeit of channeling). Rather, it is a loving relational partnership, a friendship with the divine and a willingness to pass His message along. It is a choice we make as Spirit-filled followers of Jesus. This is exactly what the apostle Peter emphasized when he wrote:

> *If anyone speaks,* **let him speak** *as the oracles of God. If anyone ministers,* **let him do it** *as with the ability which God supplies, that in all things God may be glorified through Jesus Christ, to whom belong the glory and the dominion forever and ever. Amen* (1 Peter 4:11).

His use of the words *"let him speak"* and *"let him do it"* illustrate our partnership in the matter. We are not forced by fear or spiritual power to convey messages; we are compelled by love. As believers, we are invited to convey messages of our Father's love from the spirit realm to the hearts of people on earth.

28. Clairaudience

> *Clairaudience* (n.) — This word, derived from French, means "clear hearing"; it is the ability to receive psychic impressions of sounds, music, and voices that are not audible to normal hearing.

There are times when God will speak to an individual in a voice that is audible to the human ear, but that is not the same as clairaudience. Clairaudience refers to hearing in the spirit realm with the spiritual ear. In John 4, the Bible tells us that *"God is a spirit"*; therefore, He will talk to us spiritually in our spiritual ears. Many people expect that if God, the creator of heaven and earth, is going to speak, it must be earth-shaking and deeply profound. Yet when we read the Bible, we find that God more often seems to speak very subtly and softly, such as when He spoke to Elijah the prophet.

> *Then He said, "Go out, and stand on the mountain before the LORD." And behold, the LORD passed by, and a great and strong wind tore into the mountains and broke the rocks in pieces before the LORD, but the LORD was not in the wind; and after the wind an earthquake, but the LORD was not in the earthquake; and after the earthquake a fire, but the LORD was not in the fire; and after the fire* **a still small voice.** *So it was, when Elijah heard it, that he wrapped his face in his mantle and went out and stood in the entrance of the cave. Suddenly a voice came to him, and said,* **"What are you doing here, Elijah?"** (1 Kings 19:11–13).

We can notice two things from this passage about how we hear God in the spirit:

1. God often speaks to us softly in a small voice.

Even though we might think God would speak through a strong wind, an earthquake, or a fire, He often will surprise us by talking in a still small voice.

2. God often asks questions He already knows the answer to.

Many people assume God is like a guru sitting on top of a mountain with a long white beard who only says deeply profound and mysterious things. This is not the God of the Bible. The God of the universe, who is revealed in the Bible, is our Father who loves us with all of His heart. Before the Fall, He walked and talked daily in the garden with Adam and Eve (see Gen. 3:8). And the apostle John was able to lay his head on the chest of Jesus because of the closeness of their friendship (see John 13:23).

God is very personal, and He desires to communicate with us personally, not as a mystic but as a loving father to a child. One of the ways He does this is by whispering in our ears, so to speak, in the spirit. A gentle whisper is far more intimate than a shout from a distance. This is what David, the man after God's heart, meant when he wrote, *"The secret of the LORD is for those who fear Him, and He will make them know His covenant"* (Psalm 25:14 NASB).

In Colossians, Paul also referenced the believer's ability to hear sounds (other than God's voice) in the Spirit when he encouraged the believers to use "songs from the Spirit":

> *Let the message of Christ dwell among you richly as you teach and admonish one another with all wisdom through psalms, hymns, and songs from the Spirit, singing to God with gratitude in your hearts* (Colossians 3:16).

29. Clairsentience

> ***Clairsentience*** (n.) — The ability to pick up information through the senses of smell, taste, or touch, the most common form of which includes receiving psychic information through feeling what is around you. The word *clairsentience* comes from French and means "clear feeling or sensing."

Many of the Old Testament prophets had spiritual experiences in which they smelled, tasted, or touched things in the spirit realm. For example, Ezekiel ate a scroll that tasted like honey (see Ezek. 3:3). In the New Testament, the apostle John saw and perhaps smelled the incense coming up from the prayers of the saints to the nostrils of God (see Rev. 8:3–4).

Along these lines, the apostle Paul made a statement that many Christians read as figurative. However, I believe it has literal application: *"But thanks be to God, who always leads us in triumphal procession in Christ and through us, spreads everywhere* **the fragrance of the knowledge of him**" (2 Cor. 2:14).

To some believers, this may seem very strange, yet I am convinced that the Word of God is alive and active (see Heb. 4:12), that it is available to us experientially. At times, I have literally been able to smell the fragrance of God's glory on another believer, which is exactly what Paul said should happen. This should not be considered an unusual experience.

One reality of discernment is the fact that our spirits can carry and release fragrances. For example, an individual with a strong gift of healing might smell, in the spirit, like the balm of Gilead, which is the biblical fragrance that symbolizes healing.

On the flip side, certain sins can also be discerned by smell as well. If an individual is actively involved in drug usage, a discerning believer may smell marijuana smoke in the spirit around them even though, in the natural, the person's clothing and skin may be clean at the time. Likewise, if someone has a spirit of lust heavily operating in his or her life, that person might smell, in the spirit, like musty body lotion. Those working in the adult industry typically use a large amount of body lotions that, when mixed with sweat and eight-hour days of dancing, end up smelling pretty gross. In the spirit, this aroma can be smelled spiritually as a form of discernment.

Of course, it's important to note here that if God allows us to spiritually "smell" another person, it is always for the purpose of encouraging that person or introducing freedom; it is never for the purpose of condemnation (see Rom. 8:1).

Through these examples, we can see that the New Age idea of clairsentience is an imitation of a biblical gift of discernment (in this case, particularly related to the senses) that is available to all believers.

30. Clairvoyance

Clairvoyance (n.) — This word, derived from French, means "clear seeing"; it refers to the power to see an event or an image in the past, present, or future. This type of sight does not happen with the physical eyes but with a person's inner eyes. It is also referred to as *second sight* or the *sixth sense*.

We find this type of seeing in the spirit realm throughout the Bible. Old Testament prophets commonly received their revelation this way, which is why they were often referred to as *seers* (see 1 Sam. 9:9).

In the New Testament, all believers are invited to see in the spirit realm. Jesus demonstrated this ability to see in the spirit in His encounter with Nathanael:

> *When Jesus saw Nathanael approaching, he said of him, "Here truly is an Israelite in whom there is no deceit."*
>
> *"How do you know me?" Nathanael asked.*
>
> *Jesus answered, "I saw you while you were still under the fig tree before Philip called you"* (John 1:47–48).

In other words, when He saw Nathanael, Jesus was able to access Nathanael's past through spiritual vision. This gave Him knowledge of events He otherwise could not have known about. And it convinced Nathanael of Jesus' love and lordship.

The apostle Paul prayed specifically for this spiritual sight for the Ephesian Christians:

> *Therefore I also, after I heard of your faith in the Lord Jesus and your love for all the saints, do not cease to give thanks for you, making mention of you in my prayers: that*

the God of our Lord Jesus Christ, the Father of glory, may give to you **the spirit of wisdom and revelation in the knowledge of Him, the eyes of your understanding being enlightened**; *that you may know what is the hope of His calling, what are the riches of the glory of His inheritance in the saints* (Ephesians 1:15–18).

This spiritual vision is so important to the believer that, in Revelation 3, Jesus actually rebuked the church of Laodicea for their lack of spiritual sight. Because they were looking only with their natural eyes, they thought they were doing well. Jesus charged them to ask for spiritual eye salve to anoint their eyes, enabling them to see their true condition in the spirit:

Because you say, "I am rich, have become wealthy, and have need of nothing"—and do not know that you are wretched, miserable, poor, blind, and naked—I counsel you to buy from Me gold refined in the fire, that you may be rich; and white garments, that you may be clothed, that the shame of your nakedness may not be revealed; and anoint your eyes with eye salve, that you may see (Revelation 3:17–18).

Here we see the importance of seeing in the spirit so that we may *"fix our* **eyes** *not on what is* **seen**, *but on what is unseen, since what is* **seen** *is temporary, but what is unseen is eternal"* (2 Corinthians 4:18).

31. Cold Reading

Cold Reading (n.) — A psychic reading made for someone the psychic has never met. (This is different from a Hot Reading, in which a psychic has had previous contact with the person or has a certain amount of information already about the person being read.)

What the New Age refers to as Cold Reading is a counterfeit of the biblical gift of prophecy, specifically the word of knowledge (see 1 Cor. 12:8). When people receive words of knowledge, they know some information about another person that it would be otherwise impossible for them to know. It is not information about the future; it is knowledge of facts about the past or present that are easily verifiable. Many Old Testament prophets demonstrated this gift with incredible accuracy.

One of the most striking examples is found in the life of the prophet Samuel. In First Samuel 9, a young man named Saul set out to search for his father's donkeys, which had been lost. After searching for several days, Saul and his servant came across Samuel, who knew—by the Spirit—exactly who Saul was and what he was doing. Just the day before, God had told Samuel that Saul would arrive the next day and that he should anoint him as the king of Israel. Thus, when Saul approached Samuel, asking where the seer's house was, Samuel responded with this incredible word:

> "I am the seer," Samuel replied. "Go up ahead of me to the high place, for today you are to eat with me, and in the morning I will send you on your way and will **tell you all that is in your heart. As for the donkeys you lost three days ago, do not worry about them; they have been found.** And to whom is all the desire of Israel turned, if not to you and your whole family line?" (1 Samuel 9:19-20).

Samuel, who had never before encountered Saul, promised to tell Saul all that was in his heart. That is a word of knowledge. To prove his ability, he also answered Saul's unvoiced question about the donkeys, even mentioning how many days ago they had been lost!

Jesus also demonstrated the word of knowledge in His encounter with the woman at the well:

> He told her, "Go, call your husband and come back."
>
> "I have no husband," she replied.
>
> Jesus said to her, "You are right when you say you have no husband. **The fact is, you have had five husbands, and the man you now have is not your husband**. What you have just said is quite true."
>
> "Sir," the woman said, "I can see that you are a prophet" (John 4:16–19).

Here Jesus told the woman information about her past that He could not have possibly known. He didn't do it to humiliate her but to grab her attention. Immediately she knew Jesus was no ordinary man; *"I can see that you are a prophet,"* she said. Jesus followed up His demonstration of spiritual power with a revelation of God's love for this woman that changed her life. This ability is available to all who believe in Jesus.

32. Death Omen

> **Death Omen** (n.) — According to folklore, it is a sign of an impending death. Every culture has its own unique death omens.

The death omen is really just another form of what the Bible calls prophecy—only it is specifically related to a person's time of death. Throughout the Bible, we see examples of people who knew when they were going to die. In the Old Testament, Moses is a good example of this:

> *On that same day the LORD told Moses, "Go up into the Abarim Range to Mount Nebo in Moab, across from*

> *Jericho, and view Canaan, the land I am giving the Israelites as their own possession. There on the mountain that you have climbed you will die and be gathered to your people, just as your brother Aaron died on Mount Hor and was gathered to his people"* (Deuteronomy 32:48–50).

Of course, Moses didn't simply sense his impending death because of a particular sign. He actually heard God tell him when and where he was going to die.

Jesus, too, knew when and how He would die, who would betray him, and who would kill him. He prophesied it to His disciples on multiple occasions (see Matt. 16:21; 20:18–19; Luke 9:22; John 2:18–22), and just prior to His arrest and death, He taught His disciples about the significance of His death at the Last Supper. Then, just hours before His arrest, He led them to the Garden of Gethsemane and told them:

> *This very night you will all fall away on account of me, for it is written: "I will strike the shepherd, and the sheep of the flock will be scattered." But after I have risen, I will go ahead of you into Galilee* (Matthew 26:31–32).

Through these examples, we see that the death omen is simply a counterfeit of the Christian's ability to hear specific direction about the future, including information about when, how, and where a person will die.

33. Displacement

Displacement (n.) — A lack of synchronization in psychic testing. For example, a person who, when asked to give the order of a pack of playing cards, may be one or two cards ahead or behind in sequence. Parapsychologists call displacement "psychic noise" and believe it to be caused by the absence of earth time in higher planes where psychic insight functions and the psychic association of a group of potential targets that are difficult to tell apart.

This concept of displacement is present throughout biblical prophecy and is part of modern prophecy as well. The prophet Dennis Cramer refers to this phenomenon by saying that prophecy is *discursive*, or "randomly moving from one subject to another with no particular reference to time, timing, or sequence." In other words, a prophecy may contain huge time gaps or even be fulfilled in reverse order. If a prophecy contains a particular order, it may be fulfilled in a completely different order. Because of this, even experienced prophets usually find it difficult or impossible to distinguish between past, present, and future while prophesying, and they often will not be aware of time gaps within their prophecies.[2]

We find examples of this lack of time awareness and sequential order throughout biblical prophecies. In the famous prophecy of Jesus' birth, Isaiah declared the birth of the Christ in the present tense. We get no sense of the hundreds of years that would pass between utterance and fulfillment:

> *For to us a child is born, to us a son is given, and the government will be on his shoulders. And he will be called Wonderful Counselor, Mighty God, Everlasting Father, Prince of Peace. Of the increase of his government and peace there will be no end. He will reign on David's throne and over his kingdom, establishing and upholding it with justice and righteousness from that time on and forever. The zeal of the LORD Almighty will accomplish this* (Isaiah 9:6–7).

If we had been present to hear Isaiah speak this prophecy, we probably would have thought it applied to the present, and we would have been completely wrong.

Not only does this prophecy have displacement related to the time between declaration and fulfillment, but also between the two parts of the prophecy. This passage also contains a prophecy of the establishment of Jesus' Kingdom on earth, with no indication of how many years would pass between His birth and His Kingdom. If we read it as it sounds, it would be easy to believe this prophecy indicates Christ's Kingdom would be established at the moment of His birth. However, that was not the case. Instead, we have prophetic displacement.

Another example of this is found in Romans 4:17, where Paul mentions God's ability to call things that are not as though they are:

> *As it is written: "I have made you a father of many nations." He is our father in the sight of God, in whom he believed—the God who gives life to the dead and calls things that are not as though they were* (Romans 4:17).

In other words, God actually speaks to things that do not yet exist, and through speaking, He calls them forth into reality. God called Abraham a father of many nations while he was an old man with no children and a barren wife. But God reached outside of time and began pulling Abraham into a different reality by calling him by his future identity (father of many). Because this happens outside of time (or reaches forward into the future), this sort of prophetic calling forth is a form of displacement.

34. Divination

> **Divination** (n.) — The art or practice of foretelling the future to discover hidden knowledge, find the lost, or identify the guilty by interpretation of omens or by supernatural powers.

In simple terms, divination is any attempt to communicate with the divine, to make contact with the higher spirit (supernatural) realm, or to learn the will of the gods. This concept of communicating with the divine originated at the dawn of time, when Adam and Eve regularly walked and talked with their Maker, God Almighty. Even after humanity fell into sin and experienced separation from God, the Bible tells us that God regularly communicated with people, usually through divinely-appointed prophets. When Jesus came, He opened wide the door again for all people who accept Him as Lord to communicate freely with their Father in Heaven

The counterfeit of communication with God is what is often referred to as divination; as the name implies, it is more impersonal than relational. When people attempt to communicate with the spirit world apart from Christ, they are trespassing into unprotected territory. For this reason, God commanded ancient Israel:

> *There shall not be found among you anyone who makes his son or his daughter pass through the fire, one who uses divination, one who practices witchcraft, or one who interprets omens, or a sorcerer, or one who casts a spell, or a medium, or a spiritist, or one who calls up the dead* (Deuteronomy 18:10–11).

As I discussed in Chapter 2, each of these forbidden activities involves unauthorized (and, therefore, unsafe) communication with the spirit world. They involve opening oneself up to influence from evil spirits. This is why God warned so strongly against them. God wants people to come to Him and interact with the spiritual realm through relationship with Him instead of attempting to sneak in through impersonal occult practices. God has made all this available to us through relationship with Him. He loves us that much! The apostle Paul clearly explained this when he wrote:

> *No, we speak of God's secret wisdom, a wisdom that has been hidden and that God destined for our glory before time began. None of the rulers of this age understood it, for if they had, they would not have crucified the Lord of*

glory. However, as it is written: "No eye has seen, no ear has heard, no mind has conceived what God has prepared for those who love him"—but God has revealed it to us by his Spirit. The Spirit searches all things, even the deep things of God (1 Corinthians 2:7–10).

Here we see that followers of Jesus inherit a spiritual reality and relationship with the divine that far surpasses the imitations used by those who practice divination. Through relationship with the Holy Spirit, we are invited into the deep things of God!

35. Dowsing

Dowsing (n.) — Also known as "water witching," it is performed by using a forked stick pendulum or rods to find hidden things, in particular underground water, minerals, and oil. Today it is used to locate lost objects, buried treasure, mineral deposits, and water wells, as well as to diagnose illness.

The Bible contains several references to times when a prophet used a stick to access something hidden underground or underwater. God specifically told Moses to find an underground stream in this manner:

The LORD answered Moses, "Walk on ahead of the people. Take with you some of the elders of Israel and take in your hand the staff with which you struck the Nile, and go. I will stand there before you by the rock at Horeb. Strike the rock, and water will come out of it for the people to drink." So Moses did this in the sight of the elders of Israel (Exodus 17:5–6).

In the counterfeit dowsing, a stick is used to help one find the location of something hidden. Moses' experience exceeds that. Not only did God tell Moses *where* the water was, but through the stick,

He actually caused the water to spring up above ground (through a rock, no less) so the people could drink. Why God chose to do it this way, as opposed to simply doing it Himself or having Moses command the water to come forth, I don't know. The point is, He did.

Similarly, Elisha located an ax head that had fallen into the water using a stick, and as with Moses, the miracle was not simply discovering the location of the ax head but actually causing it to rise out of the water and float until it could be retrieved (see 2 Kings 6:1–7).

36. Dream Interpretation

> **Dream Interpretation** (n.) — An ancient form of divination, based on the belief that the subconscious mind communicates with the conscious mind through dreams, that is used to discover past, present, and future answers.

Dreams are a common part of the human experience, and throughout history, people of many religions have attached great significance to them as communications from the spirit world. Here's what the Bible tells us about dreams and their purpose:

> *In a dream, in a vision of the night, when deep sleep falls on people as they slumber in their beds, he* [God] *may speak in their ears and terrify them with warnings, to turn them from wrongdoing and keep them from pride, to preserve them from the pit, their lives from perishing by the sword* (Job 33:15–18).

In other words, dreams are often symbolic messages from God, though the Bible also warns against false dreams, or dreams inspired by evil spirits (see Jer. 23:28,32; 27:9). This makes dream interpretation a pretty big deal. Not surprisingly, the Bible contains several accounts of startlingly accurate dream interpretation. In particular, two Old Testament characters, Joseph and Daniel, were expert dream interpreters who interpreted dreams for kings and influenced the course of nations. Let's look at a few examples from their lives.

In Genesis 40–41, Joseph interpreted the dreams of two men who were in prison with him—the Pharaoh's cup bearer and baker. He told them, based on their dreams, whether they would be pardoned or executed. Within three days, Joseph's interpretation came true. The baker was hanged, but the cup bearer was restored to his position. Two years later, the Pharaoh had a dream that troubled him, but none of his wise men could interpret it. Then the cup bearer remembered Joseph's gift for interpretation, and suddenly, Joseph found himself before the most powerful man in the world at that time:

> *Pharaoh said to Joseph, "I had a dream, and no one can interpret it. But I have heard it said of you that when you hear a dream you can interpret it."*
>
> *"I cannot do it," Joseph replied to Pharaoh, "but God will give Pharaoh the answer he desires"* (Genesis 41:15–16).

Pharaoh told Joseph his dream, and Joseph promptly interpreted it as a prophecy of seven years of plenty followed by seven years of famine. As a result, he was promoted to second-in-command. Over the course of the next fourteen years, Joseph's interpretation came true, and through the planning made possible by the interpretation, many lives were spared.

In Joseph's story, it's important to note that Pharaoh's false interpreters could not understand a dream that was inspired by God. Only the servant of God could interpret a dream from God. Joseph made this clear, as well, when he credited the interpretation only to God.

We see a similar pattern in the life of Daniel, who was taken as a captive to Babylon as a young boy. The Bible makes an interesting statement about Daniel and three of his friends: *"As for these four youths, God gave them knowledge and intelligence in every branch of literature and wisdom; Daniel even understood all kinds of visions and dreams"* (Daniel 1:17). As captives, they were required to undergo training in the magic arts of Babylon to become sorcerers in the king's court. Though the Babylonian sorcerers accessed demonic power to practice their arts, God used this training to gift these young Hebrew boys with His spiritual power. This is why they were able to so quickly rise above their peers to positions of leadership.

The Bible records Daniel's interpretation of several significant dreams, but I will just highlight one, which happened within the first two years of his captivity. Nebuchadnezzar, King of Babylon, had a dream that troubled him, but when he woke up, he could not remember it. He called for his magicians, commanding them to both tell him his dream and interpret it. They, of course, could not. At this, Nebuchadnezzar threatened them all with death. When Daniel heard about it, he bargained for more time and sought God for the revelation of the dream and its meaning. Sure enough, God told him the dream and its interpretation. As a result, Daniel saved many lives and was promoted to one of the top positions in the land (see Dan. 2). The dream he interpreted was a remarkably accurate prophecy of the rise and fall of four different kingdoms leading up to the birth of Christ and the advent of God's Kingdom on earth.

In the New Testament, dreams are also mentioned as a common way in which God speaks to people. Fittingly, the events surrounding Jesus' birth were full of dreams. Jesus' earthly father, Joseph, had four dreams in which he received direction for how to keep Jesus safe (see Matt. 1:20; 2:13, 19, 22). The wise men also had a dream to this same effect (see Matt. 2:12).

One of the prophecies about the advent of the New Covenant specifically lists dreams as an area of increase:

> *In the last days, God says, I will pour out my Spirit on all people. Your sons and daughters will prophesy, your young men will see visions, your old men will dream dreams* (Acts 2:17).

All who believe in Jesus have the ability to hear Him speak; therefore, they have the ability to understand their own dreams and to interpret the dreams of others. We see this in Paul's life when he received direction about where to travel on his missionary journey in a night vision (dream):

> *During the night Paul had a vision of a man of Macedonia standing and begging him, "Come over to Macedonia and help us." After Paul had seen the vision, we got ready at once to leave for Macedonia, concluding that God had called us to preach the gospel to them* (Acts 16:9–10).

In these Bible stories, we find these two facts:

1. Anyone can receive a dream from God, whether he or she believes in Him or not.

2. Only those who follow God are able to interpret dreams from Him.

Thus we can see the importance of dream interpretation! God is speaking to many people who don't know Him through their dreams, and they need followers of Jesus to help them understand what these dreams mean.

37. Extrasensory Perception (ESP)

***Extrasensory Perception (ESP)* (n.)** — The ability of some people to perceive things beyond what their five senses (sight, hearing, touch, smell and taste) can tell them. ESP is often described as a sixth sense, but it does not function like a sense and is not dependent on the other senses, age, location, time, or intelligence. It seems to originate in an alternate reality and to bring people information about the past, present, and future that they couldn't be aware of under normal circumstances.

What the New Age terms ESP is a counterfeit of the biblical ability to perceive realities in the spirit realm through the power of the Holy Spirit. It is an inner knowing that is often referred to as *discernment* or *spiritual understanding*. Jesus modeled this spiritual perception on several occasions. When the Pharisees secretly sent people to trap Jesus with difficult questions, Jesus discerned the true motive of His questioners:

> *Then the Pharisees went out and laid plans to trap him in his words.... But Jesus,* **knowing their evil intent,** *said, "You hypocrites, why are you trying to trap me? (Matthew 22:15,18)*

When Jesus made a statement that offended the theology of the religious, He discerned what they were thinking:

> *And some of the scribes were sitting there and reasoning in their hearts, "Why does this Man speak blasphemies like this? Who can forgive sins but God alone?"*

> *But immediately, when Jesus* **perceived in His spirit** *that they reasoned thus within themselves, He said to them, "Why do you reason about these things in your hearts? (Mark 2:6–8 NKJV)*

On another occasion, Jesus' disciples were worriedly discussing the fact that they had forgotten to bring bread. Jesus perceived their concern, and He used it as an opportunity to rebuke them for their lack of spiritual insight:

> *Now the disciples had forgotten to take bread, and they did not have more than one loaf with them in the boat. Then He charged them, saying, "Take heed, beware of the leaven of the Pharisees and the leaven of Herod."*
>
> *And they reasoned among themselves, saying, "It is because we have no bread."*
>
> *But Jesus,* **being aware of it***, said to them, "Why do you reason because you have no bread? Do you not yet perceive nor understand? Is your heart still hardened? Having eyes, do you not see? And having ears, do you not hear? And do you not remember?* (Mark 8:14–18 NKJV)

At another time, Jesus perceived that the crowd was about to forcibly make Him king: *"Therefore when Jesus perceived that they were about to come and take Him by force to make Him king, He departed again to the mountain by Himself alone"* (John 6:15 NKJV).

The apostle Paul also demonstrated this discernment that all followers of Jesus are called to walk in. While he was travelling as a prisoner to Rome, he sensed that they should wait out the winter in a particular port: *"Men, I perceive that this voyage will end with disaster and much loss, not only of the cargo and ship, but also our lives"* (Acts 27:10). Unfortunately, the centurion did not listen to Paul but sailed on; as a result, the ship was destroyed and the people on board survived only by following Paul's directions (which were, again, inspired by the Holy Spirit).

Also, the apostle Peter was able to discern the true state of Simon the Sorcerer's heart when he asked to receive power from the Holy Spirit:

When Simon saw that the Spirit was given at the laying on of the apostles' hands, he offered them money and said, "Give me also this ability so that everyone on whom I lay my hands may receive the Holy Spirit."

Peter answered: "May your money perish with you, because you thought you could buy the gift of God with money! You have no part or share in this ministry, because your heart is not right before God. Repent of this wickedness and pray to the Lord. Perhaps he will forgive you for having such a thought in your heart. **For I see that you are full of bitterness and captive to sin."**

Then Simon answered, "Pray to the Lord for me so that nothing you have said may happen to me" (Acts 8:18–24).

These stories illustrate well the importance of true spiritual discernment. Perhaps that is why Paul mentioned—in three different letters—praying for believers to have spiritual discernment:

And this I pray, that your love may abound still more and more **in real knowledge and all discernment**, *so that you may approve the things that are excellent, in order to be sincere and blameless* (Philippians 1:9-10 NASB).

[I pray] that the God of our Lord Jesus Christ, the Father of glory, may give to you the spirit of wisdom and revelation in the knowledge of Him, **the eyes of your understanding being enlightened...** (Ephesians 1:17–18 NASB).

We have not ceased to pray for you and to ask that you may be filled with the knowledge of His will in all spiritual wisdom and **understanding** (Colossians 1:9 NASB).

38. HOROSCOPE

> ***Horoscope*** (n.) — A diagram of the relative positions of planets and signs of the zodiac at the time of a person's birth. In astrology, a map of the heavens at a specific point in time displays the positions of the planets in the signs of the zodiac. Where a person was born is thought to be just as significant as the time of birth; the date and time determine the sun sign, but the place determines where the other planets lie on the horoscope. Astrologers interpret the positions of the various planets and their relationship to a person's sun sign to determine personality characteristics and to make predictions for the future.

The Horoscope is the counterfeit of the divine plans of God for each individual's life. As we've seen with other counterfeits of God's supernatural, the devil has taken something intended to be very personal and intimate between the Creator and His children, and he has turned it into an impersonal system and diagram through which a person can attempt to find purpose and meaning for his or her individual life apart from the Creator.

The Bible offers us a better way. Through the prophet Jeremiah, God declared to each one of us, *"'For I know the plans I have for you,' declares the LORD, 'plans to prosper you and not to harm you, plans to give you hope and a future'"* (Jer. 29:11). In other words, He has created each one of us with a unique and specific destiny. He placed us in exactly the right time period in history and location on earth to do what He created us to do. This is how Paul explained it to philosophers in Athens:

> *From one man he made every nation of men that they should inhabit the whole earth; and he determined the times set for them and the exact places where they should live* (Acts 17:26).

When we know the God of Heaven and earth, we don't need a horoscope to tell us our personality traits and purpose on earth or to predict our future. We don't need to rely on an impersonal equation to find meaning for our lives. Whether we know Him or not, we all have a Father who made us for a reason. When we know Him, He gives us so much more insight than a horoscope ever could. Then we, like Queen Esther of old, can know we were born into our specific situation and location for *"such a time as this"* (Esther 4:14).

39. Hot Reading

> **Hot Reading** (n.) — A reading in which the medium or psychic has been given prior knowledge of the person who is receiving the reading.

This is similar to Cold Reading, which we discussed previously, and it too falls under the category of the spiritual gifts of prophecy and word of knowledge described in the Bible. Here's one example of a situation when the person who prophesied (Elizabeth) had some information about the subject (Mary) but still provided information learned from the Holy Spirit:

> *At that time Mary got ready and hurried to a town in the hill country of Judea, where she entered Zechariah's home and greeted Elizabeth. When Elizabeth heard Mary's greeting, the baby leaped in her womb, and Elizabeth was filled with the Holy Spirit. In a loud voice she exclaimed: "Blessed are you among women, and blessed is the child you will bear! But why am I so favored, that the mother of my Lord should come to me? As soon as the sound of your greeting reached my ears, the baby in my womb leaped for joy. Blessed is she who has believed that what the Lord has said to her will be accomplished"* (Luke 1:39–45).

In this story, Elizabeth already knew Mary was pregnant, but she did not know the supernatural identity of the child until the Holy Spirit filled her and gave her information. Elizabeth not only prophesied about who the child was (the Son of God) but also gave a word of knowledge about Mary's response to the angel's announcement—*"may it be done to me according to your word"* (Luke 1:38).

40. Precognition or Premonition

> ***Precognition or Premonition*** (n.) — The ability to know impending events before they happen through psychic powers.

The Bible is filled with accounts of people who prophesied future events with incredible accuracy because of revelation from the Holy Spirit. In the Old Testament, this gift was reserved primarily for vocational prophets, people like Isaiah and Jeremiah. But because of Jesus' death and resurrection, now all believers are able to ask God about the future and receive prophetic information from Him. Jesus described this reality when He said:

> *I have much more to say to you, more than you can now bear. But when he, the Spirit of truth, comes, he will guide you into all truth. He will not speak on his own; he will speak only what he hears, and he will tell you what is yet to come* (John 16:12–13).

Through relationship with the Holy Spirit, we are able to know the future. This does not mean we know everything that will happen but that He can and will give us relevant insight and foreknowledge for our lives and the lives of others. Some people also receive foreknowledge about events on a national or global scale.

41. Prophecy

Prophecy (n.) — A divinely inspired vision that is a form of precognition or knowledge of the future. Throughout history, prophecies have been made through oracles, prophets, prophetesses, and psychically-gifted laypeople.

Prophecy is quite similar to some of the other topics in this section. According to the New Age definition, prophecy differs from the others because it is a visionary revelation of future events. Basically, it's a combination of precognition and clairvoyance. The Bible contains multiple examples of this, but I will highlight just one from the days of the early Church:

> *After we had been there a number of days, a prophet named Agabus came down from Judea. Coming over to us, he took Paul's belt, tied his own hands and feet with it and said, "The Holy Spirit says, 'In this way the Jews of Jerusalem will bind the owner of this belt and will hand him over to the Gentiles'"* (Acts 21:10–11).

Here Agabus delivered a prophetic word—using a physical demonstration of a vision he had seen—regarding what would happen to the apostle Paul when he went to Jerusalem.

42. Psychic Art

Psychic Art (n.) — Also known as automatic painting, it occurs when individuals who often have little or no artistic training suddenly feel overcome by a desire to drawn or paint in distinctive, professional styles. They feel guided by a spirit and may actually feel an invisible hand pushing theirs.

Divinely inspired art occurs in biblical history as well. In fact, God places such value on art that the very first person the Bible lists as having the Spirit come upon him was Bezalel, who was anointed in all kinds of craftsmanship and art in order to beautifully design the temple (see Exod. 31:1–11). Similarly, the prophet Zechariah saw a vision of four craftsmen or artists, and the Lord told him these artists would overthrow the enemies of the Lord (see Zech. 1:20–21). Though it is not clear from the vision how these craftsmen will overcome the enemy, we can assume it relates in some way to their art since they are defined as artists and not just men. Clearly, the Holy Spirit sometimes inspires artists to work in partnership with Him to create incredible works of art.

A modern example of this can be found in Akiane, an internationally-acclaimed child prodigy in both painting and poetry who paints what she sees in supernatural encounters and visions and writes poems that she receives from the Holy Spirit. She began painting at age four and writing at age seven without any formal training in either.[3]

43. Remote Viewing

> ***Remote Viewing*** (n.) — The ability to see distant or hidden objects, events, and locations beyond the range of the physical eye.

This sort of seeing in the Spirit realm, from a distance, is best illustrated in a story from the life of the prophet Elisha:

> *When Gehazi came to the hill, he took the things from the servants and put them away in the house. He sent the men away and they left. Then he went in and stood before his master Elisha. "Where have you been, Gehazi?" Elisha asked. "Your servant didn't go anywhere," Gehazi answered.*

But Elisha said to him, "Was not my spirit with you when the man got down from his chariot to meet you? Is this the time to take money, or to accept clothes, olive groves, vineyards, flocks, herds, or menservants and maidservants? Naaman's leprosy will cling to you and to your descendants forever." Then Gehazi went from Elisha's presence and he was leprous, as white as snow (2 Kings 5:24–27).

The apostle Paul also may have had this ability to see in the spirit from a distance. We see this in what he wrote to the church in Colossae: *"For though I am absent from you in body, I am present with you **in spirit** and **delight to see** how disciplined you are and how firm your faith in Christ is"* (Colossians 2:5). Most Christians read this as figurative, but I believe it's possible Paul meant it literally.

44. Retrocognition

Retrocognition (n.) — The alleged ability to know, see into, or sense the past through psychic means.

Retrocognition is similar to a cold reading, in that it involves supernatural knowledge of events or facts from the past. As mentioned before, this falls under the biblical gifts of prophecy and word of knowledge. This ability is demonstrated throughout the Scriptures, and it is promised to all who have the Holy Spirit living within them: *"But the Helper, the Holy Spirit, whom the Father will send in My name, He will teach you all things, and bring to your remembrance all that I said to you"* (John 14:26).

Some people even believe that when Moses saw the backside of God (see Exod. 33:19–23), he literally saw all the past acts of God on earth, which is what enabled him to write the first five books of Scripture, chronicling history from Creation until Moses' life, even though most of the events in those books happened before his lifetime.

45. Tapping into Ancient Truths

> ***Tapping into Ancient Truths*** *(n.)* — The belief that "hidden treasures" are reserved for those who are willing to pursue and persevere to find them.

This idea involves a pyramid-type ladder on which people must work their way up into higher truths. The process of being promoted and entrusted with deeper knowledge is based upon demonstration of one's ability to handle what they've discovered along the way. This is a counterfeit of the biblical truth of spiritual growth and maturity. When Christians accept Christ into their hearts, they are instantly forgiven of their sins and given a new nature. The Holy Spirit comes to live within them, and they are now empowered with grace from God to live righteously. Yet all believers must individually grow in their spiritual lives in God in two ways: in maturity (character) and understanding (wisdom). These are not given instantly to us but are something we grow into along our spiritual journey. The entire chapter of First Corinthians 2 talks all about the spiritual wisdom God has stored up for His followers and how we must be spiritually mature in order to receive them. Here are a few of the most relevant verses from that chapter:

> *Yet we do speak wisdom among those who are mature; a wisdom, however, not of this age nor of the rulers of this age, who are passing away; but we speak God's wisdom in a mystery, the hidden wisdom which God predestined before the ages to our glory; the wisdom which none of the rulers of this age has understood; for if they had understood it they would not have crucified the Lord of glory; but just as it is written, "Things which eye has not seen and ear has not heard, and which have not entered the heart of man, all that God has prepared for those who love Him"* (1 Corinthians 2:6–9).

This concept is also evident in the comparison of the Church to the Body of Christ, which is growing into maturity just as a natural body does:

> *Until we all attain to the unity of the faith, and of the knowledge of the Son of God, to a mature man, to the measure of the stature which belongs to the fullness of Christ. As a result, we are no longer to be children, tossed here and there by waves and carried about by every wind of doctrine, by the trickery of men, by craftiness in deceitful scheming; but speaking the truth in love, we are to grow up in all aspects into Him who is the head, even Christ, from whom the whole body, being fitted and held together by what every joint supplies, according to the proper working of each individual part, causes the growth of the body for the building up of itself in love* (Ephesians 4:13–16).

And the writer of Hebrews rebuked some Christians for their lack of growth and maturity, pointing out how poorly they had handled the truth they'd already been given:

> *For though by this time you ought to be teachers, you have need again for someone to teach you the elementary principles of the oracles of God, and you have come to need milk and not solid food. For everyone who partakes only of milk is not accustomed to the word of righteousness, for he is an infant. But solid food is for the mature, who because of practice have their senses trained to discern good and evil* (Hebrews 5:12–14).

46. Vision

Vision (n.) — A religious apparition or a vivid episode of clairvoyance. Visions generally have more clarity than dreams. Visions can be considered dreams that are had while awake.

Like dreams, visions are present throughout the Bible, and they are a tool that God often uses to speak to His people. In Numbers 12:6, God said to the Israelites, *"Hear now My words: If there is a prophet among you, I, the LORD, shall make Myself known to him in a vision. I shall speak with him in a dream."* The fact that this was considered the norm is underlined by the Bible's commentary on a spiritually-dry season in Israel's history: *"And word from the LORD was rare in those days, visions were infrequent"* (1 Sam. 3:1). Of course, God's answer for such a dry spell was to send the prophet Samuel, a man of many visions. And God continued to send Israel prophets with many visions throughout their history—men like Isaiah, Jeremiah, Ezekiel, and Daniel, as well as many others. When we page through the books of the Bible named after these men, we find vision after vision after vision.

In the New Testament, the early Christians also viewed visions as a normal occurrence. The New Testament records visions that appeared to Ananias, Paul, Cornelius, and John (see Acts 9:10,12; 10:3; 16:9; 18:9; 1 Cor. 12; Rev. 1). And the Bible makes it clear that visions will be common for those who believe in Jesus:

> *And it shall come to pass in the last days, says God, that I will pour out of My Spirit on all flesh; your sons and your daughters shall prophesy, your young men shall see visions, your old men shall dream dreams* (Acts 2:17).

47. ZODIAC

Zodiac (n.) — The system astrologers use to mark out and name constellations in the sky that the planets move through on a regular basis. The zodiac consists of an organized belt of constellations which, in western astrology, are divided into 12 signs of 30 degrees each, which encompass the stellar constellation symbolized by an animal or mythical person. These are: The Ram, the Bull, the Twins, the Crab, the Lion, the Virgin, the Scales, the Scorpion, the Archer, the Goat, the Water Bearer, the Fish.

The Zodiac is used by astrologers to predict people's personality traits and future based on when and where they were born. (For more on this, refer back to the section titled "Astronomy" in Chapter 5.)

The Bible makes mention of several constellations. In one of Job's speeches, he lists several constellations, crediting their creation to God:

> *Who alone stretches out the heavens and tramples down the waves of the sea;* **who makes the Bear, Orion and the Pleiades,** *and the chambers of the south; who does great things, unfathomable, and wondrous works without number* (Job 9:8–10).

Later, when God answers Job's complaining and questioning, He says to Job:

> *Can you bind the chains of the Pleiades, or loose the cords of Orion? Can you lead forth a constellation in its season, and guide the Bear with her satellites? Do you know the ordinances of the heavens, or fix their rule over the earth?* (Job 38:31–33)

God was saying, "This is what I do. If you can't do these things, who are you to question Me?" Clearly we see God not only knows astrology but He created the constellations and arranges them in the sky for humans to see.

The prophet Amos also credited the creation of Pleiades and Orion to God (see Amos 5:8), and the psalmist said God counts the number of the stars and gives names to all of them (see Ps. 147:4). From this we can see that God displays His wisdom and splendor in the stars of the sky for humans to see.

Chapter 7

Other Phenomenon

In this final chapter, I will highlight various spiritual phenomenon that the New Age is known for, showing how they are counterfeits of God's original design and intention for humanity. Buckle up. This is about to get weird.

48. Absent Healing

> ***Absent Healing*** (n.) — Healing resulting from the sending of healing thoughts, visualization, prayers, or energy toward some distant person or people. It is based on the belief that all beings are interconnected by a universal life force or energy and that healing thoughts send out subtle energetic charges into this web of interconnection and out to the person being thought about.

The idea of healing from a distance originated with God, the ultimate healer, who since the very beginning has used His words to create realities. When He spoke, the world was created. Thus, it is not hard for us to see how, as we imitate our Father, we can release His healing power from one location to another. God's healing power is not restricted by time or space.

The Bible verifies that miraculous healing does not always require physical contact with the sick person. Jesus demonstrated this in His encounter with the centurion in Capernaum. When the centurion approached Jesus about healing his sick servant, Jesus said, *"I will go and heal him"* (Matt. 8:7).

But the centurion stopped Him, saying, *"Lord, I do not deserve to have you come under my roof. But just say the word, and my servant will be healed"* (Matt. 8:8).

Stunned by the centurion's faith, Jesus told him, *"Go! It will be done just as you believed it would"* (Matt. 8:13). When he arrived home, the centurion discovered that at the very moment Jesus had declared his servant's healing—from a distance—the servant had been instantly healed.

The same is possible (and increasingly common) in the Church today. Often, laying hands on a person to pray for healing is not possible because of time or distance. At these times, believers can call on the healing power of God, which, of course, is not bound by time or location. As they pray in faith, they release power toward the individual in need. Prayers spoken in faith transcend time and distance, and sick individuals can be healed through prayers offered on their behalf by people in many locations.

Such remote prayer has been common throughout Church history, and it is a significant part of the modern healing movement. In fact, with the increase of technology, more and more people are receiving healing via prayers offered over cell phones, Skype, television, and even internet chat.

49. Apport

> *Apport* (n.) — The arrival of various objects through an apparent penetration of matter, or the paranormal disappearance or transportation of objects. Mediums claim to be able to produce objects from thin air or transport them through solid matter. It is also referred to as *Asport*.

This sort of activity has traditionally been shunned by Churchgoers, yet the Bible records a surprising number of instances of apport. What most fascinates me is that, in the New Age community, it is commonly understood that living objects are harder to supernaturally transport than inanimate objects. Yet the Bible gives more evidence of apports happening with physical bodies than any other object. This is just further evidence that what New Agers practice is a counterfeit of God's power. What they consider to be most difficult is, for Him, no big deal.

One of the most striking types of apport in the Bible is the transport of humans from earth to heaven without death. This happened in the Old Testament to both Enoch and Elijah. God simply "took" Enoch (see Gen. 5:24), and Elijah went to Heaven in a whirlwind (see 2 Kings 2:11). Years later, during Jesus' life on earth, Elijah actually appeared as an apport on the mountain of transfiguration, along with Moses. *"Just then there appeared before them Moses and Elijah, talking with Jesus"* (Matt. 17:3).

On another occasion, after Jesus' death and resurrection, Jesus Himself was twice the subject of an apport. First, He appeared in the middle of a conversation that His followers were having. Luke records it this way:

> *While they were still talking about this, Jesus himself stood among them and said to them, "Peace be with you." They were startled and frightened, thinking they saw a ghost* (Luke 24:36–37).

Second, Jesus appeared in a room when the doors were clearly locked. After their shock, the witnesses took the chance to touch Jesus and verify that it was in fact Him and that He had a physical body.

> *On the evening of that first day of the week, when the disciples were together, with the doors locked for fear of the Jews, Jesus came and stood among them and said, "Peace be with you!" After he said this, he showed them his hands and side. The disciples were overjoyed when they saw the Lord* (John 20:19–20).

From these instances, we can see that what the New Age calls an apport is also present in scriptural history. There's no need to fear the imitation when God can do the real thing on a much grander scale.

50. AUTOMATIC WRITING

> **Automatic Writing** (n.) — Writing that does not come from the conscious mind and is done in an altered state of consciousness. Some attribute it to spiritual beings who are somehow able to manipulate a writing utensil in order to communicate. It is also referred to as *Slate writing* and *Psychography*.

In the strictest sense of the term, *automatic writing* is "writing which is from the spirit world through an individual under the influence of a spirit." Based on this definition, the entire Bible fits the bill. It is the most perfected form of automatic writing in existence. Jesus said that His words *"are spirit and life"* (John 6:63), and orthodox Christianity has always taught that the Bible is not a collection of letters and opinions from many dead authors but that it was authored by God Himself, who divinely inspired the human authors. In fact, the Bible claims to be a living book (see Heb. 4:12) that was not written based on personal opinion but was written, word-for-word, by the Holy Spirit of God at work in individual authors. This is what the apostle Peter meant when he wrote:

> *Above all, you must understand that no prophecy of Scripture came about by the prophet's own interpretation. For prophecy never had its origin in the will of man, but men spoke from God as they were carried along by the Holy Spirit* (2 Peter 1:20–21).

Here Peter tells us how authors were inspired to write on God's behalf, saying they were *"carried along by the Holy Spirit."* Unlike the counterfeit automatic writing—in which people become a passive, unconscious tool of a spirit—the authors of the Bible partnered with God as willing and powerful agents of His grace. The Bible is a perfect document from God Himself to us. It was written not as a book of rules, but as a revelation of who God is. Thus, it is the perfect embodiment of the New Age counterfeit, automatic writing.

51. Body Work

> ***Body Work*** (n.) — Alternative medicine therapies that take into account the role of the mind and emotions in physical health and look especially at how the body interacts with the environment and universal life energies. These include therapeutic touch, CRA, acupressure, acupuncture, bioenergetics, energy balancing, reflexology, Reiki, shiatsu, and others.

The belief behind body work can essentially be boiled down to this one concept—that the mind and emotions are connected to and have a cause-and-effect relationship with the body. In recent years, this concept has been confirmed by various medical studies linking negative emotions, like unforgiveness, with illness, and vice versa. This should not be news to Christians, who have biblical revelation that humans are holistic creatures. We cannot separate our spiritual health from our emotional/mental and physical health. This is why Paul would tell his spiritual son Timothy, in the midst of spiritual council, to drink a little wine for his stomach (see 1 Tim. 5:22–23). Paul knew Timothy's physical health affected his ability to fulfill the spiritual duties mentioned in this letter.

The apostle John further confirmed this connection when he wrote, *"Beloved, I pray that in all respects you may prosper and be in good health, just as your soul prospers"* (3 John 2). This verse clearly links physical prosperity (health) with emotional/mental and spiritual prosperity. Like God, we are three-part beings, and each of our three-parts is intimately connected with the others.

When we realize this, we can see that sometimes a spiritual problem has its root in an emotional problem, sometimes a physical problem has its root in a spiritual problem, and so forth. Thus we are empowered to survey our entire being holistically and, with the help of the Holy Spirit, to understand the roots of the problems that enter our lives. We don't need methods like acupuncture or Reiki to figure this out; we simply need to ask the Holy Spirit for understanding and then listen to what He says.

52. Earthquake Effect

> **Earthquake Effect** (n.) — A phenomenon involving the room shaking as if there was an earthquake. It is usually associated with the medium D.D. Home.

The New Testament records an occasion when a room shook as if there was an earthquake in response to people's prayers. This shaking happened as people were filled with the Holy Spirit:

> *On their release, Peter and John went back to their own people and reported all that the chief priests and elders had said to them. When they heard this, they raised their voices together in prayer to God. "Sovereign Lord," they said, "you made the heaven and the earth and the sea, and*

everything in them. You spoke by the Holy Spirit through the mouth of your servant, our father David: Why do the nations rage and the peoples plot in vain? The kings of the earth take their stand and the rulers gather together against the Lord and against his Anointed One. Indeed Herod and Pontius Pilate met together with the Gentiles and the people of Israel in this city to conspire against your holy servant Jesus, whom you anointed. They did what your power and will had decided beforehand should happen. Now, Lord, consider their threats and enable your servants to speak your word with great boldness. Stretch out your hand to heal and perform miraculous signs and wonders through the name of your holy servant Jesus." After they prayed, the place where they were meeting was shaken. And they were all filled with the Holy Spirit and spoke the word of God boldly (Acts 4:23–31).

When Paul and Silas were in prison, God took this one step farther and actually caused an earthquake in response to their worship. We know this was a real earthquake because the foundations of the prison were shaken, all the chains fell off the prisoners, and the locks on the doors were broken (see Acts 16:25–26).

53. ECTOPLASM

> ***Ectoplasm*** (n.) — Derived from the Greek words *ektos* and *plasma* and meaning "exteriorized substance," it is a whitish substance that allegedly extrudes from the mouth, nose, ears, or other orifices of the medium during a séance.

Research into ectoplasm was conducted well into the twentieth century, and analyses of small pieces of ectoplasm did in some cases (although not all) reveal fraud, with the use of substances such as muslin, toothpaste, soap, gelatin, and egg white. Interest in ectoplasm has declined, but some modern mediums are still said to produce the phenomenon.

While ectoplasm, per se, is not mentioned in the Bible, something similar did happen to Saul. While Saul was traveling on the Road to Damascus, Jesus appeared to him and revealed Himself as God. A bright light flashed from Heaven and blinded Saul, who could not see for several days afterward until a Christian named Ananias came to pray for him.

> Then Ananias went to the house and entered it. Placing his hands on Saul, he said, "Brother Saul, the Lord—Jesus, who appeared to you on the road as you were coming here—has sent me so that you may see again and be filled with the Holy Spirit." Immediately, **something like scales fell from Saul's eyes**, and he could see again. He got up and was baptized, and after taking some food, he regained his strength (Acts 9:17–19).

In other words, a spiritual substance—the blinders Jesus had temporarily placed over Saul's eyes—manifested in the natural realm as physical scales or scabs. Today, Christians sometimes see this sort of phenomenon happen when people receive supernatural healing. The evil spiritual substance that was making a person ill or causing pain manifests as a physical substance when it is removed from that person's life.

54. Guardian Spirit or Angel

> ***Guardian Spirit or Angel*** (n.) — According to tribal cultures, it is a personal protective spirit that typically takes animal form. The major function of the guardian spirit is to look after its possessor and protect him or her from harm. If misfortune strikes, this is often attributed to a failure on the part of the guardian spirit, but if things run smoothly the guardian spirit is thanked.

The Bible frequently describes God as the protector of His children in the face of danger. It also tells us God has many angelic beings who serve His will on earth and in Heaven, and often these angels participate in God's acts of protection. One of the most famous passages regarding angelic help comes from Psalm 91, which is all about God's supernatural protection:

> *For he will command his angels concerning you to guard you in all your ways; they will lift you up in their hands, so that you will not strike your foot against a stone* (Psalm 91:11–12).

These verses do not indicate that specific angels are assigned to specific people but simply that angels guard us from harm. However, Jesus did indicate that each child has a specific angel (or angels) assigned to him or her:

> *See that you do not look down on one of these little ones. For I tell you that their angels in heaven always see the face of my Father in heaven* (Matthew 18:10–11).

I believe this is true not only in childhood but throughout our lives. The events surrounding Peter's supernatural escape from prison seem to confirm this. When Peter (who had just escaped prison with the aid of an angel) showed up at the house of his friends, they initially thought it was not actually him but his angel. To them, it was more believable that Peter's angel would appear than that Peter would escape from prison (see Acts 12:13–16).

55. INCORRUPTIBILITY

> ***Incorruptibility*** (n.) — Inexplicable lack of decay in a corpse, sometimes for decades or centuries after the death of the person. When no logical explanation, such as preservative methods or extreme temperatures, can be found to explain the phenomenon, some believe that supernatural or paranormal forces are at work.

We find incorruptibility at work in the Bible, most notably in the death of Jesus, who didn't decay in the grave. Though He was only dead for three days, that was enough time for a body to begin the decay process, especially in the Mediterranean climate. However, the Bible makes it clear that Jesus' body did not decay (see Acts 2:31).

This concept of incorruptibility echoes back to the creation of the first humans, Adam and Eve, who would have had incorruptible flesh if they had remained sinless. This doesn't mean their bodies would not have decayed after death but that they actually would have never died. When they chose to rebel against God, the result was the introduction of death in their physical bodies (see Gen. 2:17; 3:19). Through His death and resurrection, Jesus defeated the power of death (see Acts 2:24; Rom. 5:21; 1 Cor. 15:26) and ultimately restored to us what Adam and Eve lost. Thus, for followers of Jesus, when our physical bodies die, we will inherit immortal (incorruptible) bodies:

> *But when this perishable will have put on the imperishable, and this mortal will have put on immortality, then will come about the saying that is written, "Death is swallowed up in victory. O death, where is your victory? O death, where is your sting?"* (1 Corinthians 15:54–55 NASB).

Biblical incorruptibility is not simply a lack of decay in a corpse; it is a body that will never die. This is in the future of all who follow Jesus as Lord and Savior.

56. LEVITATION

> ***Levitation*** (n.) — The act of raising a person or an object off the ground, defying the downward gravitational pull by supernatural means.

Levitation is not something Christians talk about much, but the fact is that Jesus levitated when He walked on water, and so did Peter. *Levitate* is defined in the *Merriam-Webster Dictionary* as "to rise or float in or as if in the air especially in seeming defiance of gravitation." When Jesus walked across the stormy lake, He defied gravity in an act of levitation:

> After He had sent the crowds away, He went up on the mountain by Himself to pray; and when it was evening, He was there alone. But the boat was already a long distance from the land, battered by the waves; for the wind was contrary. **And in the fourth watch of the night He came to them, walking on the sea.** When the disciples saw Him walking on the sea, they were terrified, and said, "It is a ghost!" And they cried out in fear. But immediately Jesus spoke to them, saying, "Take courage, it is I; do not be afraid."
>
> Peter said to Him, "Lord, if it is You, command me to come to You on the water." And He said, "Come!" **And Peter got out of the boat, and walked on the water and came toward Jesus.** But seeing the wind, he became frightened, and beginning to sink, he cried out, "Lord, save me!" Immediately Jesus stretched out His hand and took hold of him, and said to him, "You of little faith, why did you doubt?" (Matthew 14:23–31 NASB).

What is most fascinating about this story is not that Jesus was able to walk on the water but that Peter could, too. It's clear from the story, and the fact that Peter fell into the water after he lost his focus, that Peter was not being "levitated" by Jesus but by his own faith. Otherwise, it would make no sense for Jesus to rebuke him for having little faith.

We also see an example of levitation when Jesus rose from the earth and ascended into Heaven (see Acts 1:9–10).

57. Miracles

Miracle (n.) — Something that happens beyond the scope of reality, typically within a religious context. Miracles are usually attributed to a divine or supernatural power that intervenes in the normal course of events and changes their expected or predicted outcome. Examples include miraculous healing and changes in weather.

The Bible is full of miracles, both in the Old and New Testaments. One of the most remarkable miracles in Scripture happened when the Holy Spirit caused Mary to become pregnant with Jesus even though she was a virgin (see Luke 1:26–35). During His life on earth, Jesus also worked many miracles, including multiplying food, calming storms, raising the dead, and so forth (see Matt. 14:13–21; 15:32–38; Mark 4:35–41; John 11).

Before His death, Jesus told His disciples that through the Holy Spirit they would be able to do all the miracles He had done and even more: *"Truly, truly, I say to you, he who believes in Me, the works that I do, he will do also; and greater works than these he will do; because I go to the Father"* (John 14:12). He also said:

> *These signs will accompany those who have believed: in My name they will cast out demons, they will speak with new tongues; they will pick up serpents, and if they drink any deadly poison, it will not hurt them; they will lay hands on the sick, and they will recover* (Mark 15:17–18, see also Matt. 10:8).

In other words, believers in Jesus should expect to do genuine and extraordinary miracles through the power of the Holy Spirit.

58. Orbs

> ***Orbs*** (n.) — Forms of energy of unknown origin that can't be seen by the naked eye but that can be seen through infrared monitors and recorded on photographic film.

The Bible records at least one instance of something like an orb appearing before a person:

> *Now a thing was secretly brought to me, and my ear received a whisper of it. In thoughts from the visions of the night, when deep sleep falls on men, fear came upon me and trembling, which made all my bones shake. Then a spirit passed before my face; the hair of my flesh stood up!* [The spirit] *stood still, but I could not discern the appearance of it. A form was before my eyes; there was silence, and then I heard a voice, saying...* (Job 4:12–16).

Here Job identifies this orb as a spirit whose form was indiscernible. Though he couldn't tell what it was, he was certain it was spiritual in origin, and it made his hair stand on end.

59. Out-of-Body Experience (OBE)

> ***Out-of-Body Experience (OBE)*** (n.) — A phenomenon in which people believe they have stepped out of or have separated from their physical bodies and have the ability to travel to other locations on earth or to non-worldly realms. It is also called *astral projection*. Approximately one in four adults believe they have had an out-of-body experience, but despite this, scientific evidence for OBEs remains inconclusive, prompting skeptics to argue that OBEs are nothing more than an altered state of consciousness.

The Bible supports the idea of out-of-body experiences, particularly those in which people travel into the heavens. One example of an earthly OBE happened in the life of the prophet Elisha, who would regularly go by the spirit to sit in the council room of the enemy king in order to hear his war plans. Elisha would then tell the king of Israel what he had seen and heard so that the king would not be caught by surprise and defeated.

> *Now the king of Aram was warring against Israel; and he counseled with his servants saying, "In such and such a place shall be my camp." The man of God sent word to the king of Israel saying, "Beware that you do not pass this place, for the Arameans are coming down there." The king of Israel sent to the place about which the man of God had told him; thus he warned him, so that he guarded himself there, more than once or twice.*
>
> *Now the heart of the king of Aram was enraged over this thing; and he called his servants and said to them, "Will you tell me which of us is for the king of Israel?" One of his servants said, "No, my lord, O king; but Elisha, the prophet who is in Israel, tells the king of Israel the words that you speak in your bedroom."* (2 Kings 6:8–12).

Here is seems Elisha could travel at will to hear what the king of Aram was planning, and he did it regularly. Similarly, the apostle Paul talks about an OBE into the third Heaven (the abode of God) in Second Corinthians:

> *I must go on boasting. Although there is nothing to be gained, I will go on to visions and revelations from the Lord. I know a man in Christ who fourteen years ago was caught up to the third heaven. Whether it was in the body or out of the body I do not know—God knows. And I know that this man—whether in the body or apart from*

the body I do not know, but God knows—was caught up to paradise. He heard inexpressible things, things that man is not permitted to tell (2 Corinthians 12:1–4).

Most Bible scholars believe Paul was describing his own experience in this passage. Clearly, he says it's possible for people to travel into spiritual realms, both in their bodies and out of their bodies. As he indicates, sometimes it is difficult to tell between the two. This is true in many of the biblical accounts of people going to Heaven or supernaturally traveling between locations on earth. Did Ezekiel, Isaiah, John, and many others go in the spirit or in the body? I'm not sure it matters. The point is that both are possible, and under the protection of Jesus, both are safe.

60. POWER OBJECTS

Power Object (n.) — Any object believed to be a source of supernatural or magical power and which confers its power to those who possess it (for example, talismans, amulets, fetishes, psychometry, charms, and crystals).

It's true. Objects can contain spiritual power and even transfer that power to people through touch. The Bible contains several accounts of God's power residing in an object.

The most astonishing example is that of the apostle Paul, who transferred the anointing to cloths that were then taken to the sick. *"God did extraordinary miracles through Paul, so that even handkerchiefs and aprons that had touched him were taken to the sick, and their illnesses were cured and the evil spirits left them"* (Acts 19:11–12). People were healed and dispossessed of evil spirits just by touching a physical object. This is indisputable evidence that physical objects can carry an anointing of power. This is not just true in the occult; it is most true in God's Kingdom.

The second example of power being carried by an object is found in the story of the bones of the prophet Elisha.

> *Elisha died and was buried. Now Moabite raiders used to enter the country every spring. Once while some Israelites were burying a man, suddenly they saw a band of raiders; so they threw the man's body into Elisha's tomb. When the body touched Elisha's bones, the man came to life and stood up on his feet* (2 Kings 13:20–21).

Resurrection power lived in Elisha's bones even though he was no longer alive. This is incredible evidence that God's power can and does reside in physical objects.

We find a third example in the story of the woman who had bled for twelve years. When she touched Jesus' garment with faith in her heart, healing virtue flowed into her, and she was instantly healed (see Luke 8:43–48). Jesus was in the midst of a crowd—being nearly crushed by all the people who wanted to be near Him. One woman, among the many who were touching Him, reached out and touched Jesus in faith. Instantly, she was healed. This is why Peter responded in disbelief when Jesus asked who had touched Him. So many people were touching Him at once, yet only one of them recognized the spiritual substance resident in even His garments and accessed that power by faith. *"At once Jesus realized that power had gone out from him. He turned around in the crowd and asked, 'Who touched me?'"* (Mark 5:30).

At another time, many people who touched Jesus' cloak in faith were instantly healed:

> *And when the men of that place recognized Him, they sent word into all that surrounding district and brought to Him all who were sick; and they implored Him that they might just touch the fringe of His cloak; and as many as touched it were cured* (Matthew 14:35–36).

Clearly, the Bible does not limit the dispersion of God's power to humans. We are the primary conduits of His power, but it is possible for our clothing or other objects we touch to also become transmitters of His power.

61. Power Spots

> ***Power Spots*** (n.) — Certain areas of the earth that are regarded as places where subtle earth energies collect. It is thought that these places possess magical or supernatural energies and are the dwelling place for spirits. These are also referred to as a *portal, vortex,* or *whirlwind.*

Christians typically refer to this reality as an open heaven, based on the story of Jacob, in which the heavens seemed to open and he saw angels ascending and descending on a ladder between earth and Heaven. While he was traveling, Jacob unknowingly spent the night at a place where there was an open heaven. While he slept, he saw in a dream the spiritual reality of that place, and God spoke to him about his destiny.

> *When Jacob awoke from his sleep, he thought, "Surely the LORD is in this place, and I was not aware of it." He was afraid and said, "How awesome is this place! This is none other than the house of God; this is the gate of heaven." Early the next morning Jacob took the stone he had placed under his head and set it up as a pillar and poured oil on top of it. He called that place Bethel, though the city used to be called Luz* (Genesis 28:16–19).

Another possible instance of an open heaven happened when Elijah was taken into Heaven. God had him travel to a specific place (by the Jordan River), and there He took Elijah up into Heaven with a whirlwind.

In Malachi 3:10, God promises to open the heavens above those who obey His Word, and in John 1:51 John said to Nathanael, *"Truly, truly, I say to you, you will see the heavens opened and the angels of God ascending and descending on the Son of Man."* When Jesus was baptized, the heavens opened above Him and the Holy Spirit descended upon Him in the form of a dove (see Matt. 3:16). And when the apostle John had his Revelation vision, he saw a door standing open in the heavens (see Rev. 4:1). All these instances of open heavens tell us that open heavens actually exist throughout the physical world.

The New Age attributes their existence to gathering earth energies. The true source of such pathways between the physical and spiritual is God.

62. Psychic Healing

> ***Psychic Healing*** (n.) — Also known as Reiki, it is a therapeutic technique that is said to involve the channeling or transfer of psychic power or universal life force through the healer to the patient. It often involves the laying on of hands and prayer, and healers claim to use psychic powers to cure illness.

Supernatural healing is another common supernatural event found in both the Old and New Testaments. Since the beginning of humanity's relationship with God, His followers have been His conduits of miraculous healing for others. The first healing in the Bible happened when Abraham healed Abimelek, king of Gerar, his wife, and his female slaves (see Gen. 20:17). Throughout the Old Testament, God anointed certain leaders and prophets to lead His people, and often their ministry included supernatural healing.

When the Israelites were about to enter the Promised Land, God clearly identified Himself as Jehovah Rapha—the Lord our Healer.

He told them,

> *If you listen carefully to the LORD your God and do what is right in his eyes, if you pay attention to his commands and keep all his decrees, I will not bring on you any of the diseases I brought on the Egyptians, for I am the LORD, who heals you* (Exodus 15:26 NIV).

When Jesus inaugurated the New Covenant, He introduced a new level and standard of supernatural healing. Malachi prophesied that the Messiah, the *"Sun of Righteousness"* would *"arise with healing in His wings"* (Mal. 4:2 NKJV), and that's exactly what He did. Everywhere He went, as He proclaimed the Kingdom, He also healed people of all their diseases and infirmities (see Matt. 4:23).

He also trained His followers to heal the sick and assumed it would be a significant part of their ministry, saying, *"Whoever believes in me will do the works I have been doing, and they will do even greater things than these…"* (John 14:12 NIV). In His mind, supernatural healing in the life of the believer is not an option but a given. Before Jesus went to the cross, He gave a commission to all who would ever follow Him. He promised His followers that certain signs would follow them, including: *"They will place their hands on sick people, and they will get well"* (Mark 16:18 NIV).

As the Book of Acts shows, the early Church lived up to that call. Through the years since then, healing has had a presence in the life of the Church. Now, more than ever before, Christians are embracing their call to heal the sick. We are realizing that, as His representatives upon the earth, we must heal others in order to represent Him accurately. If Jesus was humble, we must be humble; if Jesus healed people, then so must we. We have been empowered, commissioned, and sent as ambassadors of Heaven to bring healing to this world. If we are going to accurately represent God, we must show the world that He is Jehovah Rapha, our Healer.

63. Shape Shifting

Shape Shifting (n.) — A conscious and deliberate act of transformation from human to animal form through magical or spiritual means.

Shape shifting is a counterfeit of the biblical reality that we humans currently possess mortal and imperfect bodies that will someday (for those who follow Jesus) be changed into glorious, immortal, and perfect bodies. When people accept Jesus as Lord, a spiritual transformation takes place within them, and they literally change forms, becoming a new creation: *"Therefore, if anyone is in Christ, he is a new creation; the old has gone, the new has come"* (2 Cor. 5:17). After we die, we experience a physical transformation as well:

> *For our citizenship is in heaven, from which also we eagerly wait for a Savior, the Lord Jesus Christ; who will transform the body of our humble state into conformity with the body of His glory, by the exertion of the power that He has even to subject all things to Himself* (Philippians 3:20–21).

To foreshadow this, during His life on earth, Jesus transformed briefly into His heavenly body before three of His disciples:

> *After six days Jesus took with him Peter, James and John the brother of James, and led them up a high mountain by themselves. There he was transfigured before them. His face shone like the sun, and his clothes became as white as the light. Just then there appeared before them Moses and Elijah, talking with Jesus* (Matthew 17:1–3).

In the New Age counterfeit, people are only able to change into lower forms of existence (animals) and only temporarily. In God's supernatural reality, we "shape shift" upward into a more glorious form, first spiritually and eventually physically.

64. Spirit Attachment and Releasement

Spirit Attachment (n.) — A form of possession in which a discarnate entity attaches itself to a human being, much like a parasite. Spirit attachment is similar to possession but is the preferred term in modern times because it does not imply demonic possession.

Spirit Releasement (n.) — A form of exorcism that removes negative energy or displaced spirits from people or property in order to help correct negative behaviors and addictions. This is also known as *dispossession*. According to therapists who perform spirit releasement, "most entities are not evil or demonic but simply confused."

The Bible refers to these realities with the terms *possession* and *deliverance*. The New Age does not recognize the hostile nature of the spirits that attach themselves to humans in this way, but the Bible clearly shows that these demons mean nothing but harm for their human hosts. In fact, often during the ministries of Jesus and His disciples, they delivered people from demons in order to heal them from physical or psychological aliments. The Bible specifically recounts times when Jesus cast out demons to heal individuals of muteness (see Matt. 9:32–33), deafness (see Matt. 12:22), epilepsy (see Matt. 17:14–18), and insanity (see Mark 5:1–15). These are only the ones listed. It also says in multiples places that Jesus healed and cast demons out of all who came to Him (see Mark 1:32–39; Luke 4:36; 6:18; 7:21; Acts 10:38).

Jesus also imparted this ability to deliver those possessed by demons to all His followers, saying, *"Heal the sick, raise the dead, cleanse the lepers, cast out demons. Freely you received, freely give"* (Matt. 10:8). The disciples did this even before Jesus' death (see Mark 5:7–13; Luke 9:1–11; 10:17–20) and continued to do it afterward (see

Acts 16:16–18; 19:12). All believers are called and empowered to release people from demonic bondage through the name of Jesus and the power of the Holy Spirit.

65. Telekenesis

> ***Telekenesis*** (n.) — The movement of objects without physical intervention but through thought or will power. If the movement is intentional, it is also known as *psychokenesis*.

Telekenesis is very similar to levitation (which we talked about earlier in this chapter) except that it only involves moving or lifting objects other than oneself. Other than the example I gave under "Levitation," of the time when Jesus told His followers we can lift and move a mountain by our faith (see Matt. 17:20), we find this story:

> *The company of the prophets said to Elisha, "Look, the place where we meet with you is too small for us. Let us go to the Jordan, where each of us can get a pole; and let us build a place there for us to live." And he said, "Go." Then one of them said, "Won't you please come with your servants?" "I will," Elisha replied. And he went with them. They went to the Jordan and began to cut down trees. As one of them was cutting down a tree, the iron axe-head fell into the water. "Oh, my lord," he cried out, "it was borrowed!"*
>
> *The man of God asked, "Where did it fall?" When he showed him the place, Elisha cut a stick and threw it there, and made the iron float. "Lift it out," he said. Then the man reached out his hand and took it* (2 Kings 6:1–7).

I also referenced this story under "Dowsing" in Chapter 6. Really, it is a combination of the two concepts. First Elisha found the axe head supernaturally (similar to dowsing), and then he lifted it out of the water supernaturally (similar to telekenesis). Another amazing example of this is found in Luke 5 and John 21, where Jesus twice causes a vast number of fish to suddenly rise through the water and become caught in the disciples' fishing nets. The point is, this lifting of objects through the Holy Spirit's power is completely within the scope of what's possible for believers in Jesus.

66. Teleportation

> ***Teleportation*** (n.) — The ability to move across a distance without moving through the intervening space, typically in an instant of time.

Christians typically refer to this phenomenon of instantly traveling from one location to another as "translation." The Bible includes several stories of times when God "picked up" or moved individuals from one place to another. The Old Testament prophet Ezekiel received many of his visions in this way. God would pick Ezekiel up and take him somewhere, either to Heaven or another location on earth, in an instant. In Ezekiel 3:12–15, the Spirit of God carried Ezekiel from Babylon to Tel Abib (Tel Aviv), where he sat in the presence of the Jewish exiles for seven days, *"causing consternation among them"* (Ezek. 3:15). In other words, he was there physically, and other people could see him. He traveled there in body, not only in spirit. In Ezekiel 8–11, God even picked Ezekiel up by his hair, taking him to a series of locations to show him visions of the future of Jerusalem! The fact that He picked him up by his hair indicates this was a physical experience of being translated.

Similarly, the prophet Elijah was apparently so well-known for translating from one location to another that when Obadiah, the head of the wicked King Ahab's household, encountered Elijah along the road, and Elijah told him to get his master, Obadiah responded:

> *But now you tell me to go to my master and say, "Elijah is here." I don't know where the Spirit of the LORD may carry you when I leave you. If I go and tell Ahab and he doesn't find you, he will kill me. Yet I your servant have worshiped the LORD since my youth* (1 Kings 18:11–12).

We see translation in the New Testament, too, especially in a remarkable story from the life of Philip. After the Spirit of God directed Philip to go along a certain road, he encountered an Ethiopian eunuch who was reading a prophecy about the life of Jesus. Offering to explain to him what he was reading, Philip told the gospel story and invited the man to receive Jesus as his Lord. The eunuch gladly embraced the gospel; then this happened:

> *And he gave orders to stop the chariot. Then both Philip and the eunuch went down into the water and Philip baptized him. When they came up out of the water, the Spirit of the Lord suddenly took Philip away, and the eunuch did not see him again, but went on his way rejoicing. Philip, however, appeared at Azotus and traveled about, preaching the gospel in all the towns until he reached Caesarea* (Acts 8:38–40).

Many modern Christians have also experienced this phenomenon. Without doubt, this ability to travel supernaturally between locations at the will of God is part of the believer's supernatural inheritance in Christ. It is not something we do through magic or New Age tactics, but simply through asking our Father. He loves us, and when such supernatural travel is needed, He makes it possible to those who have faith.

67. Temporal Displacement

Temporal Displacement (n.) — Most psychics believe it is possible to travel, psychically, to any location in any time period—past, present, or future—using techniques such as meditation, remote viewing, dreaming, and out-of-body experiences. Time travel is also believed to occur in episodes of precognition, retrocognition, and bilocation.

This concept is not clearly described in the Bible, but I do believe it exists in the Bible in occurrences that are often described as Christophanies, or appearances of Jesus in physical form in the Old Testament, prior to His lifetime on earth.

One of the most well-know Christophanies happened in Genesis 18, where three men appear to Abraham, one of whom was Jesus. We know only two of them were angels because of several clues in the text. First, it says the Lord appeared to Abraham in the appearance of these three men (see Gen. 18:1–2). Second, it later says the men left and went to Sodom, but Abraham stayed with the Lord (see Gen. 18:22). We know Abraham stayed with Jesus in the flesh because the beginning of Genesis 19 tells us the two men arrived in Sodom. In other words, Jesus stayed with Abraham to negotiate Sodom's fate while the two angels walked down to the city.

Other individuals that some scholars believe to be pre-incarnate appearances of Jesus include Melchizedek (see Gen. 14; Heb. 5–7); the man Jacob wrestled (see Gen. 32:24–30); the Captain of the Lord's Host who appeared to Joshua (see Josh. 5:15); and the fourth man who appeared in the furnace with Shadrach, Meshach, and Abednego (see Dan. 3:25). From this we can see it is indeed possible for a person to travel through time. If Jesus could appear in the past as a physical being, it must mean it is possible for other humans to also transcend the usual limits of time and space.

A small number of Christians in history and a growing number today have had these types of experiences. The difference between this and what the New Agers practice is, once again, found in the source and the safety. As Christians, we do not "force" such experiences through formulas but simply follow the Holy Spirit. When He is guiding us, we are guaranteed safety no matter where He takes us.

68. ZOMBIES

> ***Zombie*** (n.) — According to Haitian and West African Voodoo traditions, a soulless, reanimated corpse resurrected from the dead by a Voodoo priest, known as a Bocor, for the purposes of indentured servitude.

Whether zombies are fact or fiction is debated among scientists and anthropologists, but regardless of their realness, we can recognize that the idea of zombies is a counterfeit of God's power to raise people from the dead.

In the Old Testament, the prophets Elijah and Elisha both raised the dead. Elijah raised the dead son of a widow back to life (see 1 Kings 17:17–24). Elisha raised to life the young son of a woman who had often provided for his needs (see 2 Kings 4:8–37). And incredibly, many years after Elisha's own death, some men threw a corpse into Elisha's grave, and when the body touched Elisha's bones, the man immediately came back to life (see 2 Kings 13:21).

The New Testament features many more resurrections—the most significant one of which, of course, is the resurrection of Jesus three days after His death on the cross (see Matt. 27:45–28:15; Mark 15:16–16:8; Luke 23:26–24:12; John 19:16–20:18). During His life on earth, Jesus also raised three people from the dead (that we know of): the daughter of the synagogue official, Jarius (see Mark 5:21–24, 35–43); a dead man who was the only son of a widow (see Luke 7:12–15); and His friend Lazarus (see John 11).

Jesus described His own ministry with these words:

> *The blind receive sight and the lame walk, the lepers are cleansed and the deaf hear,* **the dead are raised up**, *and the poor have the gospel preached to them* (Matthew 11:5).

> *For just as the Father raises the dead and gives them life, even so the Son also gives life to whom He wishes* (John 5:21).

And He also commanded His followers to do the same: *"Heal the sick, raise the dead, cleanse the lepers, cast out demons. Freely you received, freely give"* (Matt. 10:8).

The New Testament also records two instances when one of Jesus' followers raised someone from the dead. First, the apostle Peter raised the woman Tabitha from the dead (see Acts 9:36–42), and later the apostle Paul raised from the dead a young man named Eutychus, who fell out a third-floor window (see Acts 20:7–12). Clearly, believers who are filled with the Holy Spirit can raise the dead, and many modern Christians do raise the dead.

In Haiti, people live in fear of being zombified and turned into living corpses that have no self-will but are enslaved by the Voodoo priest. God's idea of resurrection is very different. He raises people into life and freedom. That's what the supernatural life with Him is all about.

Conclusion

As we have looked briefly at these sixty-eight New Age counterfeits alongside biblical realities, one major difference between the New Age and Christianity stands out. In the New Age, people must look to impersonal signs and spiritual phenomenon to connect to the spirit realm and supernatural power or knowledge about the future. This results in the development of intricate systems to create this power and connection.

By contrast, Christians look to a personal and loving God as their source for all things supernatural. They are not orphans searching the cosmos for some sense of power or belonging or meaning. They are not used by spiritual beings but chosen to partner in relationship with a good God who loves and protects them in the spiritual realms. This is the spiritual reality God intends for all people. Too many of His children have feared the supernatural and called it evil; others have mistakenly gone looking for it outside of Him. But God longs for all of us to find our purpose and experience the supernatural through a loving relationship with Him.

Endnotes

Chapter 1: Understanding the New Age Movement

1. Theresa Cheung, *The Element Encyclopedia of the Psychic World* (London: HarperCollins UK, 2010), 24.

2. Raymond Buckland, *The Witch Book: The Encyclopedia of Witchcraft, Wicca, and Neo-Paganism* (Detroit: Visible Ink Press, 2001), 510.

3. Silver Ravenwolf, *Teen Witch; Wicca for a New Generation* (St. Paul, MN: Llewellyn Publications, 1999), xiv.

4. Information on Emanuel Swedenborg taken from: *Nordisk familjebok*, 2nd edition (Swedish) "Svedberg, Jesper" (Ugglan, 1918); *Encyclopædia Britannica*, 1911 edition, "Emanuel Swedenborg"; Todd Jay Leonard, *Talking to the Other Side: A History of Modern Spiritualism and Mediumship* (Lincoln, NE: iUniverse publishers, 2005), 50–55.

5. Information on Franz Anton Mesmer taken from: Leonard, *Talking to the Other Side*, 55–57; Arthur Conan Doyle, *The History of Spiritualism* (1926), Echo Library Ed. (Middlesex, UK: Echo Library, 2006), 1–8.

6. Doyle, *The History of Spiritualism*, 21.

7. Ibid., 23.

8. John DeSalvo, Andrew Jackson Davis: *The First American Prophet and Clairvoyant* (Raleigh, NC: Lulu Publishing, 2005), 12–13.

9. Information on Andrew Jackson Davis taken from: Leonard, *Talking to the Other Side*, 57–61; DeSalvo, Andrew Jackson Davis, 12–13; Doyle, *The History of Spiritualism*, 18–27.

10. Information on the Fox sisters taken from: Leonard, *Talking to the Other Side*, 26–31; Doyle, *The History of Spiritualism*, 28–58.

11. Massimo Polidoro, *Final Séance* (Amherst, NY: Prometheus Books, 2001), 18.

12. All quotes and information regarding the meeting between Lake and Doyle are taken from *John G. Lake: His Life, His Sermons, His Boldness of Faith* (Dallas, TX: Kenneth Copeland Publications, 1994), 131–137.

13. Bob Larson, *Larson's Book of Cults* (Wheaton, IL: Tyndale House Publishers, 1987), 243–244.

14. Information on Edgar Cayce taken from: Thomas Sugrue, *There is a River, The Story of Edgar Cayce* (New York: Holt, Rinehart and Winston Inc, 1942), 336– 341; Julia Loren, *Shifting Shadows of Supernatural Power: A Prophetic Manual for those Wanting to Move in God's Supernatural Power* (Shippensburg, PA: Destiny Image, 2006), 63–66.

15. DeSalvo, *Andrew Jackson Davis*, 143.

16. Nancy Chandler Pittman, *Christian Wicca: The Trinitarian Tradition*, (Fairfield, CA, 1st Books Publishing, 2003), ix.

CHAPTER 3: POWER ENCOUNTERS AND THE OLD TESTAMENT

1. C. Peter Wagner, *Acts of the Holy Spirit* (Ventura, CA: Gospel Light, 2000), 292.

CHAPTER 4: POWER ENCOUNTERS AND THE CHURCH

1. Wagner, *Acts of the Holy Spirit*, 176.
2. Susan Garrett, *The Demise of the Devil* (Minneapolis, MN: Fortress Press, 1990), 74.
3. Wagner, *Acts of the Holy Spirit*, 399.

CHAPTER 5: ELEMENTS OF THE SPIRIT REALM

1. David Williams, *Simplified Astronomy for Astronomers* (American Federation of Astrologers, 1969), 45–56.
2. Bill Johnson, *When Heaven Invades Earth* (Shippensburg, PA: Destiny Image, 2005).
3. Chad Dedmon, in conversation with the author. Used by permission.
4. *Blue Letter Bible*, s.v. "Hagah" (Strong's H1897); http://www.blueletterbible.org/lang/lexicon/lexicon.cfm?Strongs=H1897&t=KJV.
5. William Blake, "Proverbs of Hell," *The Marriage of Heaven and Hell* (1790–1793), line 33.

Endnotes

6. *Blue Letter Bible*, s.v. "Ekstasis" (Strong's G1611); http://www.blueletterbible.org/lang/lexicon/lexicon.cfm?Strongs=G1611&t=KJV.

Chapter 6: Spiritual Insight

1. For more on the Book of Revelation, see my book *Raptureless*.

2. Dennis Cramer, *School of Prophecy: Level 1* (Williamsport, PA: Dennis Cramer Ministries, 1998), 33–34.

3. For more on Akiane, visit her website: http://www. artakiane.com/.

ADDITIONAL MATERIAL BY JONATHAN WELTON

Eyes of Honor: Training for Purity and Righteousness
by Jonathan Welton

After struggling with sexual temptation for years, author Jonathan Welton devoted himself to finding a way to be completely free from sexual sin. He read books, attended 12-step groups, and participated in counseling—with no success.

Spurred on by countless friends and acquaintances who shared a similar broken struggle and longed for freedom, the author searched Scripture. There he found the answer, which he shares with you in a compassionate, nonjudgmental way.

Eyes of Honor helps you understand how to live a life of purity by realizing:

- Your personal identity
- How to view the opposite sex correctly
- Who your enemies are

Eyes of Honor is honest and refreshing, offering hope and complete freedom and deliverance from sexual sin. Jesus' sacrifice on the cross and your salvation guarantee rescue from the appetite of sin. Your true identity empowers you to stop agreeing with lies of the enemy that ensnare you.

"This book is stunningly profound. He got my attention and kept it." **~ Dr. John Roddam**, St. Luke's Episcopal

"Jonathan has written one of the best books on being free from bondage by dealing with the root issues of sin. I highly recommend reading this book.

~ Dr. Che Ahn, Chancellor Wagner Leadership

ADDITIONAL MATERIAL BY JONATHAN WELTON

Raptureless: An Optimistic Guide to the End of the World by Jonathan Welton

What others have said...

Jonathan Welton is a voice to the rising Church. We need his teaching gift stirring the Body of Christ to action. Here in *Raptureless*, Jonathan has revealed his scholarship and ability to communicate on issues pertinent to today's Church.

~ **Harold Eberle**

Jonathan Welton has taken a bold step in confronting one of the greatest "sacred cows" of our day: end-time theology! The fear created by the expectation of a coming antichrist and a great tribulation are keeping many believers in bondage. Many believe that defeat is the future destiny of the Church. In his easy-to-read presentation, Jonathan dismantles many of the popular ideas in the Church about the end times.

~ **Joe McIntyre**

Jonathan Welton's new book, *Raptureless*, is a must read. His insights on various passages of Scripture are powerfully presented. In addition, Jonathan provides fresh historical background for a number of the historical sources that he has quoted, such as Flavius Josephus.   ~ **George Kouri**

Book TWO in the series

Book ONE: The Advancing Kingdom
Book TWO: Raptureless
Book THREE: The Art of Revelation

ADDITIONAL MATERIAL BY JONATHAN WELTON
The School of the Seers by Jonathan Welton

Your how-to guide into the spirit realm!

The School of the Seers is more than a compilation of anecdotal stories. It is the how-to guide for seeing into the spirit realm.

The fresh, profound, and new concepts taught in this book take a mystical subject (seers and the spirit realm) and make them relevant for everyday life. This book takes some of the difficult material presented in other seer books and makes it easy to understand, removes the spookiness, and provides practical application of a dimension that is biblically based and scripturally sound. Get ready to enter the world of a seer! In this groundbreaking and revelatory book, Jonathan Welton describes his unique journey in which God opened his spiritual eyes. He shares how you too can activate this gift in your life.

Discover the keys from Scripture that will help you:

- See with your spiritual eyes.
- Use the four keys to greater experiences.
- Recognize what may be hindering your discernment.
- Learn about the four spirits.
- Access divine secrets and steward heavenly revelation.
- Learn how to really worship in Spirit and in Truth.
- Understand meditation, impartation, and so much more...

ADDITIONAL MATERIAL BY JONATHAN WELTON

Normal Christianity: If Jesus is Normal, what is the Church? by Jonathan Welton

Jesus and the Book of Acts are the standard of *Normal Christianity*.

Remember the fad a few years ago when people wore bracelets reminding them, What Would Jesus Do? Christians state that Jesus is the example of how to live, yet this has been limited in many cases to how we view our moral character. When Christians tell me they want to live like Jesus, I like to ask if they have multiplied food, healed the sick, walked on water, raised the dead, paid their taxes with fish money, calmed storms, and so forth. I typically receive bewildered looks, but that is what it is like to live like Jesus!

Perhaps we are ignoring a large portion of what living like Jesus really includes. Many Christians believe they can live like Jesus without ever operating in the supernatural. After reading in the Bible about all the miracles He performed, does that sound right to you? (Excerpt from book)

What others have said

I believe before Jesus returns there will be two churches. One will be religious, and the other will be normal. This book of Jonathan Welton's will help restore your childlike faith, and you will become normal!

~ **Sid Roth,** Host of It's Supernatural! Television Program

Aurora Writing & Editing Services

Amy Calkins is not only a dear friend, but also a tremendous writer and editor. I have had the pleasure of working with her on four of my books, and she is a gift of God. I would strongly urge anyone to work with her; she will help you take your writing to a whole new level.

—Jonathan Welton

AMY CALKINS,
WRITER & EDITOR

Writing an effective and influential book is not as simple as typing up your ideas in a book-length document and sending it off to the printer. Getting a book into print is easier now than it's ever been due to the growth of low-cost self-publishing and the powerful communication tools available through the internet. Yet the ability to craft a well-written and effective book still takes time and expertise. That's where Aurora comes in. Let us help you craft your ideas and message into a form that will have the ability to influence and inspire. Whether through ghostwriting, copyediting, or proofreading, we want to help your book succeed. For more information on what these services entail, as well as endorsements from authors we've worked with, visit aurora-pub.com.

WWW.AURORA-PUB.COM